JURISDICTIONS

Take Charge of The Sphere You Influence

What leaders are saying about this book.

In 'Jurisdictions' Joye Knauf Alit gives us a practical guide to engaging in spiritual warfare by what we speak. Through biblical accounts and her own experiences, Joye brilliantly demonstrates how to have divine authority over our sphere of influence. The pages are filled with informative, interesting and powerful insights into the dominion God has entrusted to us. We too have a role in bringing the kingdom of God into our own jurisdiction. We have watched Joye fight the good fight of faith for the last thirty five years. Joye is our friend and an awesome warrior for the Lord.

Heidi G. Baker, PhD
Co-Founder and Director of Iris Global

Joye Alit is a veteran intercessor. I am delighted that she has written about her many years of experience, and especially about how we ordinary followers of the Lord through His grace and empowerment can operate with the authority of Heaven to bring about His healing and transformation in the jurisdiction He has given to us. This is what Jesus meant when He told us to "occupy till I come". May many read this book and be inspired to use its valuable insights to bring the beauty and flavour of Heaven to the place where they live and work!

John Robb
Chairman, International Prayer Council
International Facilitator, World Prayer Assembly 2012

For the last 25 years of our ministry journey, we have had the joy of sharing many life and ministry experiences with Joye Alit. Joye is a remarkable servant of God, marked by her devotion to Jesus, her pioneering spirit and her perseverance no-matter-what. And Jurisdictions is a remarkable book, borne of intimacy with Jesus, uncompromising obedience to God's will, a beautiful grasp of the realm of the Spirit and a deep knowledge of world affairs, interpreted through a lens of spiritual blessing and curse. The powerful personal stories and unfolding Biblical insights provide a strong, inspiring foundation for this 'prophetic' book which has shades of the writings of the Apostle John in his mature years.

Colin and Judith Noyes
CoachNet Global/South Pacific Region

I'm so thrilled that this book has come into being. The church has great need of it. We are at a time in history when the world is expecting that those who claim to belong to God will actually demonstrate His power and authority. A book such as this can only be birthed from a place of deep intimacy and devotion to Jesus Christ Himself.

Joye Alit is a woman who clearly knows God in a powerful way. She exudes a glory which can only be attributed to her experiential knowledge of a quality relationship with Him. No wonder He confides in her – she is His friend, both qualified and authorized to represent His truth and His plans. I heartily recommend this book as a life-shaping revelatory vehicle into the greater Christian dynamic.

Dr Lynne Hamilton,
Founder/Leader Forerunners International Network.
Founder/Leader Women's Apostolic Alliance.

Joye has written a very helpful and timely book opening a rite of passage for the reader into a mature understanding of Jurisdiction. Our words and declarations bring kingdom authority to confront the powers of darkness. Taking responsibility through kingdom principles in our God given jurisdictions makes us people of great influence. Jesus changed the course of history by His words, and empowers us to follow His example. Thank you Joye.

Apostle Dr Royree Jensen
Rivers Apostolic Centre & H.I.M. Australia

The knowledge in this book by Joye Alit can make the difference of life and death to you. (Proverbs 18:21.) Words are a powerful creative force.

Joye adds another dimension to this in her book 'Jurisdictions' by helping you find the territory or sphere of influence that God has given you jurisdiction over, i.e. the legal right to speak or decree over. This book is life changing and Joye speaks from a place of intimacy with the Lord and many years of experience in spiritual warfare.

Pastor Barbara Miller B.A. (Hons Psych) MAPS, Gr Dip Sociology.
Author, Co-Founder Centre for Reconciliation and Peace

Thanks for this timely message that is critical right now regarding the revelations of the Glory dawning upon us here on planet earth.

In her book 'Jurisdictions' Joye Knauf Alit defined jurisdiction as the area over which you have legal right to speak, and the area God has portioned you influence over. Joye also explained with demonstrations from examples of her own life and popular biblical characters like Joseph in Egypt and Queen Esther in Persia. She devoted a whole chapter on how to exercise authority over one's jurisdiction like Jesus did.

The Church at large, as the ruling council (ecclesia) of God on earth, has failed to exercise her authority over her jurisdiction for the last two thousand years. As a result, we have never seen the Kingdom of God manifested on earth in that time. But with the Glory of the Lord arising over the nations now, heralding the Day of the Lord, our understanding of our God-given jurisdiction has become critical for the Kingdom of God and our survival on earth. 'Jurisdictions' is a very timely message for the Church right now.

Apostle Milo Siilata,
All People's Prayer Assembly; Deep Sea Canoe Movement, Pacific.

The Book is coming out in GOD'S perfect timing and is of great import to the Body, as the HOLY SPIRIT is calling the LORD'S Warrior Bride to take Her place in the Vanguard of MESSIAH'S Army that is offering Herself freely in the Day of His Power.

The book is Divinely Inspired and bears the seal of God's pounding heartbeat. Indeed 'jurisdiction' is such a great word; as Zion Christian Ministries came to understand once you had spoken it into our midst. We are immensely grateful to you and the Lord.

Noel Mann
Founder Zion Christian Ministries

I am blessed how beautifully Joye has brought this wonderful book to us explaining the truth about the jurisdiction in our sphere of influence. I am sure that reading this book would be an eye-opening for many of us and many would be highly benefited.

Rev Dawa Singye Bhutia
Founder/Director Himalayan Good News Network

Joye, the whole book is great – takes us into a different dimension – the one we should be living in all the time! C.S. Lewis captured a lot of it in the Narnia series, but even that falls far short of the reality of what God is creating and where we stand as His Bride!

Gwyneth Priestly-Ward
Missionary and Translator for Erave people, PNG

Jurisdictions Take Charge of the Sphere You Influence
© Joye Knauf Alit 2016
Jubilaté Publications. Queensland, Australia. jubilatemin@gmail.com

jubilatemin@gmail.com
jurisdictions4you@gmail.com
Cover concept by Joye Knauf Alit and Lyn Mackie
Cover Design by Book Whispers
Typesetting by Book Whispers

Images:
© Eraxion | Dreamstime.com - City - Skyline Photo
© Cugianza84 | Dreamstime.com - Persian Empire Map (detailed) Photo
Author photo by AliciaT DeZine Photography

National Library of Australia Cataloguing-in-Publication entry:
Creator:	Alit, Joye, author.
Title:	Jurisdictions : take charge of the sphere you influence / Joye Knauf Alit.
ISBN:	9780994573605 (paperback)
Subjects:	Good and evil.
	Spirituality.
	Spiritual warfare.
	End of the world--Biblical teaching.
Dewey Number:	231.8

Unless otherwise noted, all Scripture quotations are taken from THE MESSAGE © 1993, 1994, 1995, 1996, 2000, 20001, 20002. Used by permission of NavPress Publishing Group. Scripture quotations from the following versions of the Holy Bible are also used: NKJV - New King James Version © 1982 Thomas Nelson, Inc, by permission. NIV - New International Version © 1973,1978,1984 International Bible Society, by permission Zondervan Publishing House. NLT - New Living Translation © 1996, 2004, 2007, by permission Tyndale House Publishers Inc., Carol Stream, IL 60188. All rights reserved.

All rights reserved. No part of this publication may be reproduced, stored in a retrieval system or transmitted in any form by any means without the prior permission of the copyright owner.

JURISDICTIONS

Take Charge of The Sphere You Influence

Joye Knauf Alit

*You must influence them;
do not let them influence you. (Jeremiah 15:19 NLT)*

Dedication

I dedicate this book to the cloud of witnesses
on Heaven's balconies cheering us on —
heroes of faith not complete without us.
Still waiting.

Acknowledgements

My heartfelt thanks goes to my King for loving and never giving up on me. He kept on talking even when I didn't. Thanks for interjecting and keeping me on track with what You wanted said in this book.

And to those wonderful friends, including family, who read too-early drafts of an incomplete manuscript, but discussed them anyway, helping me heaps. For many hours of editing, and fitting me into the publishing rules (even getting caught up in the spiritual fray and overcoming), thankyou Gwyneth and the friends who had to come to your aid. Caleb and Lyn I'm so grateful for your valuable artistic gifts. To God's precious generals who were willing to endorse what I wrote, I humbly thank you. Annie, and Rochelle at Book Whispers guided me through a maze of back lanes till suddenly I have burst into print after 77 years of dreams. That's an achievement! We have invested together in the invisible Kingdom and anticipate the moment when it too will burst into view and every eye will see. I love you all.

I want to also acknowledge the great men and women of God who over the years have invested in me, made invaluable deposits from Heaven into my spirit, taught me and formed the person I am today. Great Pentecostal pioneers who stayed in our humble home when I was a child: 'Grandpa' Valdez Snr, pioneer of AOG, New Zealand, who later took me under your wing. Donald Gee, Howard Carter, David DuPlessis, William Burton (who pointed me to Africa). Uncle Elton Knauf, my missionary inspiration, martyred there.

Voice of Healing was my bread and butter, fed to us by Mum to supplement our daily scripture diet at family devotions — priceless heritage. Thankyou Tommy Hicks, AA Allen, William Branham, Oral Roberts for coming to New Zealand and so impacting me, especially your week of miracles Skierski. Thank you, Ian Hunt. And thanks, Dad, for dragging us kids in the car all over the country all hours of the night to be under these ministries. What a privilege!

And my own dear Grandad, AW Thompson, apostle to AOG in the early days. My precious Māori friends, especially of the Ngati Tuwharetoa, King Country, who taught me so much. Len Jones, Fred Jarvis, Dal and Dorothy Walker, Moma Devin, Oh Tjie Sin, Caleb bin Ibrahim, Cecil Mulvagh (who gave us a home church), Mel Tari, Terry Philips, Rolland and Heidi Baker and the Toymaker team. My Bali village family who embraced me and taught me the value of community and to enjoy simplicity. (I keep trying to replicate it in Australia, but we don't do community like you.) Shared rooms with Gwen Shaw, Beth Alves. Thankyou Garnet Budge, who became a father to me when I left the foreign mission field to a foreign home one. Olive Gates who provided me a bolthole, thank you. Tom Inglis who helped me set a worship life-style and introduced me to a newly emerging Rick Joyner. And Rick, though we never met in person, what an affirmation and inspiration you have been, giving me permission to accept things I was seeing. My dear friend Judy Noyes (who tries to keep me grounded) who with Ben Gray introduced me to evolving Prayer Movements world-wide. Beloved Pacific Island friends Paul Sikele and warriors, as well as Milo Siilata and Prophet Michael Maeliau. Noel Mann and your flock for powerful spiritual support. Cindy Jacobs you taught me so much — Brisbane, Jerusalem, London. What a strategic learning curve warriors John Robb, Kjell Sjoberg, Leslie Keegel and team took me on, followed by other great national prayer leaders. Brian Mannion you taught me the power of ACCEPTANCE. Beloved Beres Bartlet (one can't meet you and not be impacted) for deliberately investing in me. Prophet

Debra Gaborit, I value more than I can say the years you gave me. Prophet Lynne Hamilton, thank you.

Thank you to the intrepid friends who have joined me on journeys into spiritual war zones, and those who stayed behind and prayed, sometimes copping shrapnel. To my daughters and sons-in-law and Henare who consistently speak into my life, showing up stuff and opening new horizons. You teach me heaps. And all the other wonderful people who, though not named here, have been written into my life and contributed to who I am. We are all part of each other and without any one of you I wouldn't be the same, nor you without me – and this book.

(I wanted to keep this to a page, but how can I?) You have made me so rich and I am most grateful to the Lord for each of you, some in the cloud already, men in white linen, 'souls of just men made perfect', urging us on. **We're coming!**

~

Contents

Acknowledgements		vii
Introduction		xiii
Prologue	In the Body or out of the Body?	xvii
Chapter 1	Jurisdiction	1
Chapter 2	So What's Your Jurisdiction and what can you do about it?	7
Chapter 3	Especially For Kids	25
Chapter 4	Other Jurisdictions And Examples	34
Chapter 5	Who Is In Charge Here?	43
Chapter 6	Who Is In Charge Here – Baal or Yahweh?	54
Chapter 7	Take Charge: Joseph the Dreamer	71
Chapter 8	Take Charge: Esther the Orphan	77
Chapter 9	Your Diction In Your Jurisdiction 'Speak the Word Only'	91
Chapter 10	"Learn To Do Authority Like Jesus Did"	101
Chapter 11	Your Juris In Your Jurisdiction	108
Chapter 12	Requisite For Reigning – Romance	129
Chapter 13	The Culmination 'And Then I'll Marry You'	139

Introduction

Did you know you have your own personal jurisdiction?

I didn't. But after all we're 'Kings and Priests' so it goes with the territory! We're citizens and heirs of a spiritual Kingdom – which we all pray will be established 'on earth as it is in Heaven'.

I discovered everyone has a jurisdiction. My jurisdiction is totally unique to me and yours is totally unique to you. You have a sphere around you which you influence. Everyone has. This is your God-assigned jurisdiction.

So I invite you through these pages to sit down and chat about this revelation. Let's see if we can discover what your jurisdiction is and see how significant you are to God in His great plan of the Ages.

It's a progressive revelation and I don't profess to have it all. No one does. So I'd like to open a dialogue, a three-way one, you and me and God. Who knows what God will share with you? We each enrich one another, and collectively we complete God's ultimate dream.

I am excited about the possibilities of this revelation, and you will be too as we explore it together. God had a purpose in giving you your sphere of influence – He wants you to establish His 'dominion' (His Lordship) over it. He is the Lord of everything and we are His Regents here on earth. It's the same old command He gave to Adam: 'have dominion'.

If we take a look at the definition of Jurisdiction we will get a better handle on what it means for us.

Juris – has to do with the law, something legal.

Diction – (root word: dikté) is about speech or words.

So our jurisdiction is the area over which we have the legal right to speak.

The ***diction*_ary**[1] says jurisdiction is:

a. *(Concrete noun) The territory over which authority is exercised.*

b. *(Abstract noun) The right, power or authority to administer justice.*

That means we have a Territory – the sphere of influence God gives us; and a Right – to speak and administer justice.

This book is about your jurisdiction – the territory over which you have the legal right to speak or make '*pronounce*_ments'. That's pretty impressive – the sphere over which you can legally dikté, or pronounce.

Remember the words of the centurion to Jesus? "No, Master, you don't need to come to my humble home. I too am a man under authority and I also have authority. I say (dikté) to one 'do this', to another 'go there' and they do. So, Master, speak the word (dikté) only and my servant will be healed." (This Roman foreigner, an officer of the forces occupying Israel at the time, had an astonishing understanding of the spirit realm and the authority Jesus had in it. He also understood the enormous power in words, especially words backed up by God's legal system!)

Taken aback, Jesus said, "I've yet to come across this simple trust in Israel, the very people who are supposed to know all about God and how He works. This man is the vanguard of many outsiders who will be coming from all directions ... sitting down at God's kingdom banquet alongside Abraham, Isaac and Jacob ..." Then Jesus turned to the captain and said, "Go. What you believed could happen has happened." At that moment his servant became well. (Mt 8:10–13)

You and I are some of the 'many outsiders' who have come into God's Kingdom and to whom this great privilege has been given. What you believe can happen, will happen. Speak the word only.

---

1 http://www.eudict.com/

I wonder, if God's people had actually taken dominion over the jurisdictions He has given us, moved in the right and authority he gave us to 'administer justice' ('you in your small corner and I in mine'), how much more territory His Kingdom may have been occupying by now.

This book is not about formulas to get what you want from God.

> It's about restoring to our beloved King His rightful inheritance.
>
> It's about finishing the work He began and for which He paid such a price – a work to which a great host of witnesses cheers us on.
>
> It's about completing the faith of all the great men and women of faith who have gone before and who are not complete without us.[2]
>
> It's about the culmination of God's glorious dream.

Its purpose is to help you:

1. identify your jurisdiction
2. understand your position as an heir
3. know the authority God has vested in you
4. accept the responsibility we have as 'sons' to bring things into alignment with the culture and values of Heaven
5. to inspire you to 'take charge' of your jurisdiction.

So, I pray that this chat will help bring clarity and motivate you to take charge of your particular jurisdiction – for His sake.

Always wanted to change the world? That's because Father wants you to and has provided all you need to do it.

Come with me on an exhilarating journey and marvel at how much transformation we can bring when we accept responsibility for our jurisdictions.

And be prepared for a surprise destination – a secret revealed at The End!

~

---

2 Heb 11:40

Prologue

In the Body or Out of the Body?

It was a sunshiny Autumn day in 2003. A stillness settled over me so I came inside and sat quietly on the sofa with the Lord. I was remembering a prophecy stating that some of us here would be transported to see in the heavenlies. I believed I was to be one.

"Now would be as good a time as any," I whispered to the Lord.

Immediately there seemed to be a bustling around me – of angels? Were they getting ready to carry me off? If this was going to be an out-of-body experience, what did I do with my body? I wondered if I should lie down. "Just make yourself comfortable," was the impression.

Then we seemed to be flying across my valley – and away. I couldn't make out anything particular until we were approaching mountains, zooming in to one particular triangular peak (rather like the stylized mountains featured in Chinese art). This was My Mountain. It was very steep and, clinging to its upper reaches, was My City. It wasn't a big city and it wasn't gold. It seemed to be white and silver and light. I can't explain how the streets didn't seem to be steep.

I strode up the street, heading for the summit feeling comfortably at home. It was my city. Although to my knowledge I'd never been here before, I had a cosy feeling of being totally accepted and wrapped in the embrace of my home town. Not only was it my home town, but I had the sense that I was totally in charge. Children tumbled out of houses and clutched onto my hands, welcoming me as 'Mama'. I picked up one child, then squatted to chat to another. I called her 'Luh', the term of address for a little Balinese girl. That surprised me. I was remembering Isaiah 49 which the Lord had long ago given me – *'and these, where had they been?'* I had always thought of those children as being Māori from my New Zealand years in the Revival. It hadn't dawned on me that I had Balinese children as well. There were a few adults hovering in the background, all part of my 'family', welcoming me.

I strode on up the road as though I knew where I was going. Everyone followed, or ran on just ahead of me. I was aware that angel escorts were off on the fringes, letting the crowd take over for now. We emerged from the houses and there was the summit like a small ridge – very bright white. The focal point was a Throne. I gasped and fell at the knees of the white-robed person on the throne, overjoyed to see him. (My mind, outside the vision, was buzzing over this. If I was so surprised to see him, this wasn't the Lord then?)

The man in white linen stood up and put his arm over my shoulders showing me range after range of mountain peaks. All this area was ours. There were shiny silver citadels on each of the mountains. "Places you've taken," he said. If that were the case I was eager to know what further mountains needed taking. He pointed out dark ranges waiting to be conquered behind his throne. He seemed to be showing me what had been done and what yet needed to be done. I had a sense that the next dark place I was to bring under the jurisdiction of the King was far to the north – as though we were somewhere equivalent to the Himalayas (without any snow!). But of course it was a spiritual location. It was my home base, and very high.

I became aware that this 'home base' was where I returned for refreshing and strength. I was in need of it now before attempting to do battle for those territories still in darkness, the mountains he had shown me that were still to be taken.

Suddenly a shaft of light streamed down from heaven like a huge funnel connecting the two realms, forming a portal. I began to shake and cry. The glory cloud surrounded me and somehow, instantly, I was in another place.

I was splashing and playing in the pool of a Fountain. But – simultaneously – I was drinking at the Fountain, and at the same time I was delighting in the fine shower of the Fountain. I can't tell you how all that happens at once, but this realm was not confined to earth-bound time-space rules. I was aware that the Fountain was the Lord; these were all aspects of being in Him.

Then He took a person form and, like a mother taking a child out of the bath, He was wrapping me about in a gossamer light-filled 'towel', drying me off. This material became a shimmering robe as he wrapped me in it. I looked down at the robe and discovered my arms too were like gossamer, my whole being shimmering with Light. He wrapped me in His arms drawing me to Him. And I dissolved into Him! I disappeared into Him and we were one – no longer separate entities.

I had longed for this depth of intimacy. Now I could KNOW that I was in Him and He was in me. It wasn't me any more. Now I could truly interface people with Jesus.

I opened my eyes – and I am here in my lounge room on my local mountain looking out over conquered territory under our jurisdiction and rule – the Lord's and mine.

As a result of this journey in the spirit I received a download of understanding on two new topics – about Jurisdictions, and about Intimacy. In the following chapters I will attempt to pass on to you some of these revelations.

~

Chapter 1
Jurisdiction

Your jurisdiction is the area over which God has given you influence.

Everyone adored him. Mums loved him, little children chortled for him, even the teens followed him about smitten with awe, and the dads hung around chuffed to be in his company. He was more like a friend than a sovereign. Daily the King walked among them, listening to their stories, delighting in their company, playing with the children. He knew each name. Every individual was important to the King and they knew it. They were in awe of his majesty and wisdom and could implicitly trust his justice. Under his sovereignty the wheels of life turned harmoniously and everyone felt secure and cared for. Need was unknown.

One day the King left on an extended journey to visit his other realms. He left his sons in charge of his empire, allocating them provinces to rule and administer in his place. His sons' responsibility was to see that the kingdom continued to run in the way he had established it and to protect its citizens, its land and life, its wealth and borders.

When at length the King returned, he was deeply saddened to find numbers of his sons living lavishly indulgent lives. They showed no concern for the kingdom or the welfare of its citizens. Borders were broken down, law and order was no longer enforced. The country was savaged by enemies who were robbing, killing, and destroying the beautiful kingdom. Their intent was to dispossess the much-loved King and subjugate His territory.

Long before Time was or the world was formed, God dreamed of you. When He moulded the mountains, traced the rivers, filled in the oceans and wrote the local history He had you in mind. Then He carefully crafted you with all the special attributes you would need for the territories He planned for you in His great blueprint. Your destiny is irrevocably entwined with where He places you, fitting neatly into your own specific landscape (physical, spiritual, social) at the precisely designed time.

We all have a jurisdiction, a sphere of influence. This is part of the spiritual inheritance granted to us over which we are to establish the Lord's dominion. Over our particular jurisdiction we have the legal right to speak and to administer the rule of God's kingdom. Our job is to re-establish and maintain the rule of the King – His dominion. (In chapters 10 and 11 we will discuss the characteristics of this upside-down kingdom.)

Dominion

I found the definitions of 'dominion' to be fascinatingly relevant for us in this context of establishing the Lord's dominion in our jurisdictions.

Did the name 'Adam' cross your mind at the mention of 'dominion'? It seems to have at <*vocabulary.com*>[3].

> 6. Dominion (abstract noun):
> *When you are in charge of something or rule it, you have 'dominion' over it. The most famous use of the word occurs in the Christian Bible, when God grants people dominion over ~~other~~ animals*[4]. *(Gen 1).*

---

3 www.vocabulary.com/dictionary/dominion
4 Strike-through mine

Right of course! I love that their immediate thought is of Adam and GOD with relation to Dominion because '*His is the Kingdom, the Power and the Glory*'. This is definitely the right focus!

In Eden's garden, Adam and Eve were allocated the first Jurisdiction. Just think about the following definition for a moment:

A king has dominion over his kingdom. Dominion implies power – even absolute power.

Note: the King has 'absolute' power over His Kingdom. Psalm 24:1 states clearly that '*the earth is the Lord's, the world and all that live on it.*'

Note too that Psalm 115:16 states that the earth He has given to the children of men.

7. Dominion (concrete noun)

A dominion can also be an area or territory controlled by a larger country or state.

Exactly. This book is all about **taking spiritual territory**. A 'Dominion' is a Territory. The territories we are taking are brought under the dominion of a larger, and far superior, Kingdom.

Here's an inspiring exercise. Read slowly this list of synonyms for '*dominion*' (abstract noun), savouring each one as an attribute of our Father, the King.

Sovereignty, control, supremacy, ascendancy, command, rule, direction, government, jurisdiction, lordship.

This is the worldview He wants us to operate from.

And see if this doesn't make you feel cared for and secure – some synonyms for the concrete noun '*dominion*':

dependency, protectorate

The territories we take here on earth are *outposts, provinces* of the Heavenly Kingdom which we are helping to *colonise*. ('*Be fruitful and multiply.*')

Google[5] enlarges on the definition:

a. Dominion (abstract noun):

---

5 www.google.com.au/dictionary.reference.com/browse/dominion

The power or right of governing and controlling; sovereign authority.

We have been given the *legal right* and the *power* to govern and control our jurisdictions.

b. Dominion (concrete noun):

A territory in which a single rulership holds sway.

This Territory – is under a **single rulership,** *a sovereign authority.* It has:

- no board of governors
- no multiple leadership
- no democratic confusion

The Territory comes under:

One undisputed Sovereign Ruler

to whom is all honour and praise and glory forever

endlessly into infinity.

This Ruler is

absolute Good,

absolute Love,

absolute Life,

absolute Joy,

absolute Peace,

absolute Justice ,

absolute Knowledge,

absolute Wisdom…

He is the absolute of every positive attribute. He is the author and source of them all.

That's how it was in the Beginning:

"Here you are Adam, earth is your Territory. Take dominion," God said, "over everything around you. Govern on My behalf. I am the Sovereign; you are my Regents. See that all my Goodness flows lavishly to every part and every cohabitant of earth. Enjoy!"

Imagine for a moment what it was like before the Fall. Adam and Eve knew God, walked with Him daily, explored His creation with Him and knew His heart. There was only good, only positive, only harmony. There were no contentions, no disturbances, no limitations, no insecurities. There was no death, or decay, or deterioration, or degeneration.

But we know the sequel. The tired old story (Gen 3) is that they gave up their authority, abdicated their role in their jurisdiction. In following the direction[6] of someone else they put themselves under a rival rule. They handed over their inheritance like Esau. We still continue to struggle with the effects of that.

It's pretty sobering how, in a thoughtless, self-gratifying instant, we can lose so much – with irrevocable consequences.

Enter death, sorrow, strife, pain and their menacing friends – into Paradise. Enter war, the incessant battles between two kingdoms: Good versus Evil, Light versus Darkness. This is an unrelenting spiritual war, not against flesh and blood, but against principalities and powers and rulers of wickedness.

So Adam bombed out. But God had a plan. He had you in mind!

Have you noticed how, starting in Genesis and right through scripture, the constant cry of the Father's heart is, *'that they would know Me!'*[7]

"I'll do this and then they'll recognize Me."

"I'll do that, then they'll acknowledge Me, then they'll know I Am God."

But His children persistently ignored Him. Hurt, maybe God reasoned like this, "I am a spirit. They can't see Me. They're limited now to the physical, so they can't see and recognize Me. I'll give Myself a Body."

So, God came, in a body like us, and became 'Adam the Second'. He wrested back dominion and, at great cost, established His new Kingdom. Now, every one of us born into His Kingdom has a mandate to see that this Kingdom takes root and expands to once again encompass the whole earth. Be fruitful and multiply, bringing many sons into glory. It is the precious

---

6   a synonym of Dominion

7   Here are a few of the instances: Ex 10:2; 16:12; Ezek 6:7,14; 7:4,27; 11:10,12; 12:15,16,20

inheritance of the Son. He deserves it. It is my passion to take back territory – 'give me this mountain!' – so I may present it back to its rightful King.

It's not a visible kingdom; it's a spirit kingdom. We are only temporarily in physical bodies which are just houses for our spirits. God's dominion is to be established first in the spirit realm, then we will see it begin to manifest in the natural realm around us.

There's just one Ruler and Owner and our job is to bring the territory back under His rulership. So, **dominion is the territory being ruled by the rightful King.**

Your Jurisdiction is the territory granted to you over which you have the legal right to speak and the mandate to bring under this dominion.

~

Chapter 2
So What's Your Jurisdiction
and what can you do about it?

"I'm just a common labourer," you say, or "I'm just a mum at home. I don't have influence anywhere." Or "I'm just an old pensioner stuck in the house and no one listens to me anymore." Or "I'm just a kid at school and no one even respects me."

Well, I have news for you: if you're born into God's Royal Family, the Holy Spirit in you is just as awesome and powerful as He is in Billy Graham, or Heidi Baker, or whoever your spiritual hero may be. He doesn't diminish to get into you, no matter how small you think you are! And, wherever you are, you are the King's Regent, representing Him around you. *I am giving you the same work that I have been doing... Just as the Father sent me, I send you.* (Jn 14:12; 20:21)[8]

Think about those pre-Fall days, the way God created everything in the beginning. He's actually paid exorbitantly for things to be returned to that condition. That's how they are in the Kingdom He's made us citizens of, His invisible spiritual Kingdom where we live. He wants you to bring that atmosphere to the earth-place where He's put you.

---

8 See also: Mt 28:18 Lk 9:1

Mums/Dads at Home

So you're a stay-at-home Mum or Dad (a 'Home Executive', a 'Family Supervisor') and think you don't really qualify for a Jurisdiction. Well, let's just think about it for a minute. Your home is yours (even if you only rent it). You have the legal right to run it the way you want – to say who comes in and who doesn't, what takes place there, what the atmosphere is like. For instance: the children take their shoes off at the door; they don't traipse mud through your house and mess your carpets. The dog stays outside; he's not allowed in. You don't allow bad language, bad attitudes, or smoking inside.

That's exactly how God wants you to administer your spiritual jurisdiction. You put out a welcome mat for things you want to come into your home; you

Keep out!

Some years ago a Global Multi-faith Festival was planned for my town. National prayer leaders advised me that we should 'pray it out', 'shut it down'. Somehow I didn't feel this was what the Lord wanted. Indeed, why shouldn't He, the Light, the Life, the Truth, the Way, come out far and away the most desirable, powerful and glorious in a display of all religions?

Since this was our Jurisdiction we planned to deal with the Festival in the following way: We defined the boundary over which we were establishing God's dominion. Then at every access point to the area we prayed and symbolically sprinkled a blood line across the road forbidding any spirits from the kingdom of darkness to cross that line. ("This is territory Jesus died to redeem.") People may enter, but spirits associated with them were forbidden entry and must drop off at that point. This meant that the different faiths presenting had no spiritual power to lure or deceive, or to manifest any supernatural powers.

As well, we saturated the venue with prayer and the presence of God, worshipping there beforehand and maintaining a continuous inconspicuous presence of praying worshippers exalting the One True God.

The result was an informational festival without a heavy spiritual atmosphere, and Jesus got positive airtime. He was the greatest!

Although the event was billed a success no further such festivals could get off the ground.

shut the door to things that are not acceptable.

Spiritual dirt will contaminate your home and your family – keep it out. In Matthew 16:19 and 18:18 the words 'bind' and 'loose' mean 'allow' and 'disallow'. You're establishing God's Kingdom in your home. In the Spirit speak out over your territory what you disallow. (You are speaking into the spirit realm; no one else needs to hear you.)

Fill your home with God's Presence and His character so that everyone who walks over the threshold senses Him. They have stepped into your jurisdiction which you have placed under His dominion and everything not of Him is shut out – dropped off at the gate! You are making your home a Heaven zone, and anything inappropriate must drop off.

Have you visited places where you have suddenly felt an almost tangible sense of peace? You feel pleasantly surrounded by a comforting atmosphere of well-being. You sense you can reach out and just about touch God; He seems so near. I believe this is a tiny bit of heaven breaking through on earth. And you can create something similar in your jurisdiction. God wants earth back!

Speak over your children

Sally couldn't sleep. She was afraid to because her sleep was plagued by terrifying dreams. In the night she would creep sobbing into Mum and Dad's bed, snuggling in for protection. After some nights Mum and Dad became impatient with this behaviour and sterner with their daughter. They didn't want the invasion of their bed becoming a habit. This only made things worse. They lay nightly listening to their little girl's stifled sobs and occasional screams and thrashing as she succumbed to sleep and yet another attack.

They decided they needed to take spiritual authority over what was happening to their daughter. While she was at school they entered her room, anointed her bed and the door and windows symbolically with the oil of the Holy Spirit and a dab of wine, symbol of the blood of Jesus which defeated Satan's stuff. They forbade any dark thing to enter or to any longer torment her. They spoke peace and security, sweet dreams, contented sleep, and filled the room with the presence of heavenly beings – the atmosphere of Heaven. Sally never again complained about frightening dreams.

Speak over your children and bring them – and anyone who enters – into alignment with God's agendas and attitudes. Your children are yours to form for the future – a huge and vitally important part of your jurisdiction and you will never know how far your influence may reach through them. Disallow the evil one to tamper with them, or to stunt or cripple their spiritual growth, or divert them onto wrong paths. Set them apart to God and His purposes for their lives, and make that a rule in the spirit realm. You have the legal right to speak God's purposes over them. In fact, it is your God-given responsibility. You also have the right to speak over the lives of all those you engage with, especially those coming into your house.

Now, because this is an exercise of the spirit and establishing a spiritual kingdom, you don't have to make these proclamations aloud and, in fact, no one need ever know except you and God.

> **Important:** this is not witchcraft and we are not manipulating people. We are speaking into the spirit realm. We must only speak God's agendas over people and align them with His Kingdom purposes. That's not hard. God wants everyone saved and to come to a knowledge of the truth. Speak God's truth over their lives, His revelation, His blessing, His will (not yours!) You can **disallow man's agendas, political agendas, demonic agendas, and align people with God's agendas** (not what you think is right for them). In this way you do not have to make the judgment as to what God's will is in specific situations. Your aim is to bring heaven to earth – Thy Kingdom come, Thy will be done, on earth as it is in Heaven.

Two Mums-at-Home who Impacted the World

Esther Ilnisky

> *I was praying in my bedroom when my three-year-old daughter, Lauren, came in and lay on the floor next to me. I asked her to leave because this was my time with the Lord. The Holy Spirit immediately checked me, that I should teach her everything I had learned, and to include her, because her spirit is the same as mine. So I told her she could pray with me. She prayed the most profound prayer I've ever heard. She is now eight and still at it!*[9]

Elizabeth Kotlowski recounts how Esther herself learned to pray:

> *At three years old she daily invaded her mother's bed-cum-prayer room, crawling over her mother's prayer tools – piles of magazines, clippings from newspapers, maps of the world. She tells how she cried when her mother cried, rejoiced when her mother rejoiced, and when her mother's heart danced, she danced on the piles of papers. The generations were linked in that prayer closet and out of it grew a world prayer movement.*[10]

Ivy

> *From the time she was an infant, Ivy's mother took her into the prayer closet with her for her daily routine intercession. As Ivy began to talk, she drew her into intercession, asking her to pray with her. She guided Ivy and asked her what God was saying to her heart. She expected Ivy to hear from God, received what she had to say, encouraged and nurtured her.*
>
> *When they drove together to town, Ivy joined her mother in*

---

9   Esther Ilnisky, Let the Children Pray, pp34-35. Regal, 2000
10   Elizabeth Kotlowski, Let the Children, 2007

praying for everything from family to the people driving by. Even playtime became a prayer time when, playing with her Barbie dolls, mother would suggest it was time for prayer, and she and Ivy would pray with Barbie and Ken. So Ivy's mother has mentored her daughter who, at ten, is now a powerful prayer warrior and passionate lover of Jesus.[11]

Grandparents

If you are still on planet earth you're not past your use-by date here, whoever you are (or think you aren't!). You may feel useless and unable to make much contribution around you, but you are here for a purpose. You have a jurisdiction and God wants you to keep ruling it. You still have all the backing of Heaven as you administer your sphere of influence. Every one of your descendants, the 'fruit of your womb', is under your jurisdiction and blessed. Lock them into God's plans for their careers and their life-mates. Forbid the enemy to divert them onto destructive tracks. Keep declaring God's promises over them. Remember the Lamb was slain for the whole household that night in Egypt. Families are priority in God's agenda.

How many stories have you heard of praying grandparents? "My grandmother took me to church." "My Grandmother used to pray for me …"

I hope you're beginning to realize that whatever your occupation, and wherever you work or study, or spend your time, you have a sphere of influence and you can bring that environment under the Lord's control.

My grandparents had ten children. They were all brought up in a godly home and were involved in what God was doing in their area. The first four went full time into God's service, the middle two became pillars of their churches, the last four slipped away from their faith, and their parents grieved but prayed continuously. They had established a rule in their jurisdiction: every one of their children was an indisputable part of God's inheritance and belonged to Him. It wasn't until some years after

---

11 Fischer, Redefining Children's Ministry, p168. 2005

Grandad and Grandma had shifted to their heavenly home that the last of their children returned to active faith. All ten eventually became citizens of God's Kingdom on earth, the last of them just relocating to heaven last month. That must have been a grand reunion! Be encouraged.

Elderly or House-bound

I love the story of the old lady kneeling alone in her room, hands clasped praying. At the same time, half way around the world, a lone evangelist was walking down a dark village road delivering tracts to the thatched homes. The old lady, still in her praying position, was now hovering over the darkest hut in that remote village. The evangelist knocked and a surly man took the tract, closed the door and threw the tract on the table. But at the moment the door had opened the old lady entered, still in her praying position. She began at floor level to lift the darkness. Little by little it began to rise, until it reached the level of the man's eyes. He glanced at the table, reached out and began to read the tract. The old lady kept on with her weight lifting, pushing the darkness up clear of the man's head and on towards the ceiling. As it reached the roof the man knelt to the floor and accepted the Light of the World. At that moment the darkness disappeared through the roof and the old lady was back in her room rejoicing at the victory won in prayer.

You have no idea how far afield your influence is impacting, and you may not have even left your own home. Think of those who come to you – the tradies, the service providers, the salespeople. I remember chatting with a tradie who had come to the house. He left, backing away and saying, "Whoa, that was really powerful that what you just said!" I had to stop to recall. We were talking about the woes of the world and I said something about putting our trust in Jesus, "… after all, He's coming back to rule the world." He left reeling with the impact of an encounter with the Truth. I've never seen him again, but he came into my jurisdiction and I continue to speak God's destiny over his life.

Tradies

Or maybe you're one of those whose job takes you into homes. Recognize those homes as part of your divinely appointed jurisdiction. Take the Kingdom and the presence of the Comforter with you. Leave the atmosphere changed – and charged – when you leave. You have brought Life (the One Who lives in you) into the home.

Jenni writes:

My husband and I ran a plastering business. We committed each day to the Lord, declaring our desire to 'take the land' and bring the atmosphere of heaven wherever we were working that day, specifically asking for opportunities to witness for Him.

We were asked to quote on repairing holes in walls made during a burglary. The lady, Maria, nervously pulled posters off the walls revealing holes – some a metre high. They were in both the living area and the hallway – about eight in all. She accepted our price and we arranged the day for the job. 'Those holes were not made by a break in,' Eddie said as we drove away. We had also sensed darkness in the house.

As we set up for the job on the day Maria was agitated. 'I can't do this. I am so stressed.' I put down my bucket and put my arm round her. 'Maria, whatever is wrong?' She burst into tears, saying her husband worked overseas, she couldn't handle the two boys and she had a very responsible job. I asked if she had any Christian beliefs and she said she had prayed to Mary but nothing changed. But yes, she would like us to pray for her. 'We are not praying to Mary or the saints we are going to ask Jesus to help you,' Eddie said. He prayed a simple prayer for protection and peace then she had to leave. Minutes later she was back to ask if we could stay until she came home at 4.00 pm so she could talk.

Maria returned amazed at the peace she'd experienced all day. It was her 16-year-old who had made the holes. He didn't want to go to school. We were able to tell her that, as Youth workers, we had counselled several children from that school. Our advice was to let him have some time out and see if there was a change. We talked to her about Jesus having the answers to her dilemmas.

When we arrived next morning to finish the work she was waiting for us to pray for her before she went to work. David was staying home as we'd recommended. Eddie, as he worked, kept talking to him about the Lord, eventually leading him in a prayer of repentance and inviting the Lord into his life.

Maria came to our home the following Sunday to see Derek Prince's How to Pass from Curse to Blessing. At the end she immediately stood up and fervently prayed the sample prayer. David had completely changed, she said; he was not going back to the school but would do a TAFE course.

Maria turned out to have two doctorates, one in Psychology and the other in Psychiatry. She told us that she had taken a whole room full of study books to the tip as it was all rubbish and the only answer was Jesus, whatever her clients' religion. She had already started to tell them this and pray for them with remarkable effect.

The Lord used holes in the wall to gain access into a house that never had visitors – so that He could reach a lady and her son who desperately needed Him.

So the presence of the Truth they carried even emptied out the library. Hilarious!

Jenni continues:

A Ceiling Repair Turned to a Spiritual House Cleaning

> As we set up for the morning's repair job on a damaged ceiling our client, Lola, settled into an easy chair for a social day. We chit-chatted about the weather, the state of the nation and the world. Eddie finally interjected with the question, 'Do you believe in miracles?' She believed in the supernatural, she said. Eddie descended the ladder and from his wallet showed Lola pictures of a baby with the disfiguring disease known as 'fish scale'. It is incurable. The photos showed the child progressively improving until his fingers were free, his skin much improved and his eyes no longer blind. Eddie said simply, 'That was a miracle.'
>
> Lola shared that she was learning to be a tarot card reader, that reiki and card reading were part of her life and that she had just bought a new set of cards. We worked and talked the rest of the day, silently calling Lola's spirit out of deception. The next day we returned to finish the job and left her with the Derek Prince video, 'From Curse to Blessing'.
>
> Later that afternoon around 4.30 there was a knock at our door and, to my surprise, there was Lola. She informed me she had watched the tape, prayed the prayer of salvation, broken the curse, renounced her involvement in Freemasonry and occult, been to the Christian Bookshop, and bought a Bible and a picture of Jesus to hang in her room. Also she had dumped the tarot cards, instruction books and even the table they had been resting on. The interesting thing was, she felt she had to put the bin right off her property on to the street. Her query now was, 'What do I do now I have decided to go with the good guys?' A few days later we prayed through her house anointing it with oil and dedicating it to the Lord's work.[12]

---

12 Jenni Trevatt by permission

Sequel, Lola now runs her own Bible Study group. She has led many people to the Jesus and into deliverance and the Baptism of the Holy Spirit – all the result of tradies taking dominion in the territory where their job led them.

Wherever You Are You're An Interface

Because you are a God-carrier, a house for the Holy Spirit, wherever you go you carry Him. Whoever you meet, therefore, you interface with Him. In other words, everyone you meet or connect with is also meeting up with the Spirit of God – coming smack up with Him. Wherever you go and whoever you meet enters your sphere of influence and comes under your jurisdiction. You have the legal right to speak God's Kingdom dominion over their lives. Have the attitude of Jesus towards those you contact: *The Kingdom of God has come to you*. Be aware that you are interfacing them to the spirit world. *We live and walk in the Spirit.*

At the Hairdresser's

The last haircut I had was destiny-making! The hairdresser's 7-year-old popped in from school.

"That's an interesting name, Levi," I said. "How did he come by that name?" I was wondering if my hairdresser had Jewish connections.

"Oh I don't know, we liked it. I think we chose it before he was born."

"A priestly name," I mused.

"Oh really?" There was definitely a spark of interest in that tone.

"Yes, Levi was one of the twelve tribes of Israel and they were the ones chosen to be the priests. The Levites led the worship in the Temple and taught the people how to relate to God."

"He's always been very compassionate and wanting to help people. He was late for class last week trying to get a little girl up from the ditch. What did you say about the Temple?"

"They led their people in Worship in the Temple."

"Yes, he's definitely a leader."

I was acutely aware that the Holy Spirit was sowing into this mother's heart a picture of her son's destiny. She was accepting my words and believing that what she had named her son was in fact his destiny. From now on she would perceive her son differently and be open to God's direction for his life. I was elated knowing that I had been speaking God's destiny over that little boy's life. They had interfaced with the Holy Spirit.

You Are Not Insignificant

So 'common labourer', mum, grandpa, grandma, child or oldie – whoever you are and wherever God has planted you – you are not insignificant. You have a jurisdiction. You are absolutely vital to your jurisdiction, because it is totally unique to you. Start taking charge of it and see what God will do.

Following are two true stories about children – a little girl and her father, and a little boy and his mother – a boy and girl who are not even named. But their lives were so significant in God's Kingdom that they have been commemorated for 2000 years.

These stories are highly significant for every one of us who have children in our jurisdictions.

~

GIVE THEM SOMETHING TO EAT

A Little Girl

Her father was a community leader and a church elder, weighed down with all the responsibilities and problems of his jurisdiction. But he had one agonizing problem he didn't know what to do with. It was not a church or a community problem that burdened him so much. It was a family problem.

(How many of us in public life have a secret problem gnawing at us in the background – a personal problem?) The man's only child – his beloved 12-year-old daughter – was dying. You can read the story in Luke 8:49–56.

Jairus, not knowing what else to do, came to Jesus. "Please Master," he begged, "can you please come and heal my daughter?" Jesus agreed and they began their halting way in the direction of Jairus' home. There were so many needs, all pressing on the Master for attention. Could He not sense how urgent this was? In the end, before they were even near the house, Jairus received the news he was dreading.

"Don't trouble the Master," the servant said. "There's no use His coming now. She's past the point of no return. She's beyond help. She's DEAD."

Jesus contradicted the news. "She's not dead," He said and continued on. When the Master and His followers at last arrived, the family and friends were weeping inconsolably. The professional wailers were lamenting loudly. "What a tragedy!" "So young!" Jesus dismissed all of that. He picked just three of His disciples, ones He knew really believed Who He was. (*You are the Christ, the Son of the Living God.*) They followed the distraught parents to the bedside.

(When you have a problem, whether a civic one or a family one, take Jesus to it and surround yourself with positive, believing people. Get rid of those who speak death and discouragement. There is no 'point of no return' to God; there is no situation beyond His help. Take Him right to it.)

Jesus **spoke** to the girl – His 'diction'. It was His jurisdiction – area over which He had legal right to speak – not just because He was God, but because He was invited by the father of the girl. She sat up – alive. *Life and death are in the power of the tongue.*

Jesus gave her back to her parents. "**Give her something to eat**," He said.

Can you hear the Spirit of God crying out today: "This generation is not dead. Give them something to eat; they are starving!"

Many of our children today have been neglected and left to starve. They are starved of attention and love, affection and respect, affirmation and guidance; their spiritual bread has been denied them both at home and in their schools. In some cases the Bread of Life has been deliberately kept from them, stolen and destroyed. Parents consumed with work and self-interest have left children to their own 'devices', and they have starved – even of the basics for a healthy soul, to say nothing of a healthy spirit.

Had Jairus been too busy with his church community and activities? For sure he loved his daughter, but was she dying of neglect because he had too many other commitments and not enough time to give her spirit food?

God is saying loudly today: Give the little children something to eat – something nourishing, something that feeds life to their spirits. They're not dead, they're hungry.

Parents, Pastors and Youth workers, the case of the children and youth out there is not hopeless. Don't write them off. They are not dead. But they soon will be if they are not fed. They are ill and starving on the junk food the world feeds them – starving for healthy spiritual food in your jurisdiction.

Lamentations 4:3,4 sets up a lament on this very issue. *Even wild jackals nurture their babies, give them their breasts to suckle. But my people have turned cruel to their babies, like an ostrich in the wilderness. Babies have nothing to drink. Their tongues stick to the roofs of their mouths. Little children ask for bread but no one gives them so much as a crust.*

As each night watch begins get up and cry out in prayer. Pour your heart out face to face with the Master. Lift high your hands. **Beg for the lives of your children who are starving to death out on the streets.** (Lam 2:19) Hear the Holy Spirit crying out for the children of this generation:

"Give them something to eat!"

~

A Little Boy

The chapter following the story of 'the little girl' (Jn 6:5-13) tells a story about 'a little boy' who was fed. (These nameless children were not 'big names' or celebrities. They were ordinary everyday children.)

Jesus was testing His disciple Philip's faith saying: "How can we feed all these people?"

Philip blustered like any of us would: "5000 men, let alone women and children; probably 20,000 mouths! It would cost the earth to buy just bread – and what village would have that much bread – especially at this time of day? And even if we could get it from, say, several villages, the twelve of us couldn't carry that much. It's just not practical to even think about it."

Poor old Philip, always the logical, practical one. He was locked into the boundaries of the natural world he'd always lived in. Philip lived in his head, like most of us, rationalizing everything. Jesus was pushing his boundaries, trying to let him catch a glimpse of another realm: a super-natural kingdom.

Andrew came to the rescue. "There's a little boy here. He's got 5 loaves and 2 fish."

How do you think Andrew knew what was in the child's lunch? Had the little boy at their elbows heard Jesus' challenge, nudged Andrew and showed him his lunch pouch – offering his contribution?

"But how silly of me," stuttered Andrew, "how could that possibly help? There are thousands of people. I don't know what possessed me to even mention it." Andrew was embarrassed when he thought about it, his practical mind clicking back in. What was it possessed him? For an instant it had seemed almost possible – must have been the earnestness of the little boy.

Jesus smiled approvingly at the little boy and held out his hand. "Bring them here." The boy came eagerly and handed over his lunch, proud that he could supply something Jesus wanted. (You too have something valuable

Jesus needs.) Jesus reached an arm around his shoulder which said, "You're on my wavelength, young man. They haven't got a clue, have they? But you get it; this isn't limited to the natural realm. You can see something else, and as a reward I'm going to show you more than you ever dreamed."

Jesus took the lunch his Mum had prepared him, breaking up his little damper breads and the two fish she had so carefully packed. He handed baskets of the food to the disciples. "Pass it out to everybody, make sure they all get some. There's enough for everyone." **Give them something to eat.**

Did you ever think about the little boy's Mum? She provided a generous lunch for her young son – five breads – knowing that he'd probably be out all day. She let him go off on his own, knowing where he'd be. He'd be following Jesus, and she let him go. She provided food for him and let him go. (Mum, if you provide the right food for your boy or your girl, you can let them go. They'll be following the Master.) Hers is a significant unsung role in this story.

When Jesus says, "How can we feed all these people?" the answer is, "A little boy" – a little boy who has been fed by his mother – 'given food to eat'.

That little boy fed at least 20,000 people that day. Jesus is still saying, "How are we going to feed all the people?" and the answer is the same – "a little boy". In God's plan for these End Days, children (with something to eat) are **the answer to the needs of the hungry multitudes.**

On the day God spoke to me from these stories my daily Psalm reading underlined His message.

> *He planted a witness in Jacob, set His Word* (the Bread) *firmly in Israel, then commanded our parents to teach it to their children so the next generation would know and all the generations to come – know the truth and tell the stories so their children can trust in God, never forget the works of God, but keep his commandments to the letter. Heaven forbid they should be like their parents, bull-headed, bad, a fickle and faithless bunch who never stayed true to God ... it was clear they didn't believe God,*

had no intention of trusting in His help. (Ps 78:5-8, 22).

God **commanded** parents to teach their children the stories and the commands. It wasn't an option, a choice, a nice thing to do, or a silly old-fashioned thing to do; it was a command from God. *'Tell the stories of God's great acts – past and present, for others and for you. And don't undermine the words by your actions or lifestyle displaying your lack of belief and trust. Such inconsistent words become poison bread, bringing death.'*

Prayer:

Lord, forgive us! We have not obeyed You by diligently teaching our children your commands and how to obey them, nor have we filled their lives with the stories of your great deeds. We are guilty of spiritual child neglect. As a result we have a generation of very sick children. Heavenly Father, we cry to you for forgiveness and ask that you will show us ways to rectify our wrongs and to reach and heal our children.

If you have children in your jurisdiction – these stories are for you. The Christ in us is a Life-giver. Feed the children and the needs of the multitudes will be met.

It is the time of the Child in God's kingdom purposes.

~

Chapter 3
Especially For Kids

Dear Reader, This chapter is written to share with children. If you have young ones, read it aloud to them. Let older children read it for themselves by lending them your book. If children are not part of your life you can skip to the next chapter to pursue your own jurisdiction. However you will definitely be inspired by some of the stories of children acting with the authority of the Holy Spirit.

Kids at School

"Just a kid at school," you think, but there you are, with a full-size Holy Spirit living in you! You think no one respects or listens to you? Wait till they're confronted with the One Who lives inside you! The spirit world around you recognizes you and knows Who that is in you. God really wants His Kingdom to come in schools. That's why He's put you in that school with that jurisdiction – to speak His plans into it. You didn't know God had specific plans for your school? Ask Him, and then speak them into being, because He's given you that ability.

Quietly, in the Spirit, begin to speak and shut down stuff you know gets God upset – abuse, bullying, rebellion, injustice, harmful things like drugs and drink and porn and promiscuity, anti-God (antichrist) attitudes and teaching. Try it. In fact God **expects** you to. Open the classroom or the school up to good influences, peace (for example: "In the Name of Jesus I open up this school or classroom or playground … to God's Peace … I call in and welcome God's peace, etc … Thank you, Lord, for your peace filling up all the atmosphere in my school …"). Invite harmony, compassion, openness to the Gospel, faith – and hey, why not miracles? Bind the spirit of unbelief in Jesus' Name; tell him he's not welcome. Keep doing this even if you don't see immediate results, because it is having an effect in the spirit realm. Jesus in you can create a 'magnetic field' around you that tugs at people's spirits and makes them want to know God, because you carry Him and they're interfacing with Him when they relate to you. You have something their spirits are hungry for.

Find someone else at school who loves Jesus and join forces, pray and declare together. *One puts a thousand to flight, but two chase off 10,000!* (Deut 32:30) All sorts of things can begin happening. You're changing the atmosphere, starting to establish God's dominion in your jurisdiction.

Is there a Christian club at your school? If not, start one; I did. I invited visiting international speakers to come and speak at school at lunch times. Other times we met and discussed our Bibles and prayed together. 'Meet at the Pole' started in one school where the kids gathered at the flagpole to pray at lunch break. It's spread around the world. 'The Call' is another youth movement sweeping the world where kids are stepping up to the plate and beginning to influence their surroundings for God's Kingdom. (See how many others you can find online and learn what they do.)

Kawerau, New Zealand

As I write (2014), exactly this is happening in a small milling town in New Zealand. The town has been infamous for its gang warfare, drugs and violence. Some High School kids met on the field to pray. God's power fell on them, tears and repentance and intercession broke out. The group grew daily. Kids are now constantly meeting in twos and threes around school to pray for specific needs and they're seeing miracle answers – healings, runaway kids returning home …

Parents began to ask what was going on. Meetings started in the School hall, now running four nights a week. Up to 600 people have attended. Gang members and leaders are coming to the Lord with deep repentance. Reconciliation is happening. Youth and police and gang members are praying for one another in God-huddles. The Headmaster admits a quarter of his school is now a 'Jesus kid' and whatever is happening is only good; he wants it to continue. The council, courts and police are all impacted and thrilled with the change happening in their town, willing to help in whatever way they can. The fire is already spreading to other towns.

Primary School Tree Meeting

It was lunch break and I needed a 'secret' place to teach my friend more about Jesus. Perched up in the trees lining our school drive we read our Bibles and prayed for other friends to 'get saved' too. The Headmaster decided to take a stroll down the drive. We huddled in breathless silence as he marched beneath us and back again his gaze fixed forward. We knew he had seen us but he never reprimanded us for tree-climbing. We thought it best, though, to find a venue that didn't break the rules. To my delight I have recently discovered a friend who gave her heart to Jesus in answer to our prayers all those years ago. She's been serving Him passionately ever since.

Of course school isn't your only jurisdiction. There's your home and family, and relatives and friends and neighbours and street and sports friends, even your city or your nation as you'll see below. You mightn't have thought so, but you have influence and the Holy Spirit in you wants to touch all those you come in contact with. Pray for them; ask God what He wants for their lives and declare and speak it over them. If you don't know, just declare God's plans come to pass in their lives.

Other Fires Lit by Kids

There are lots of examples of school children igniting revivals that have not only influenced their school, but extended to their town and community and to whole nations.

Malaysia

The Kelabit people in Serawak, Borneo are an example. One of the students in class began to weep as she was touched by the Lord, next thing the whole class was weeping. It spread to the whole school and classes had to be suspended. The children cried out to God to forgive their sins, and for their families and their people. The Churches were affected (became infected!) and everyone began to weep to God in repentance. Children began preaching along with adults because the Holy Spirit was on them. Soon the whole 'people group' was fully following the Lord. For a whole generation every Kelabit person was a passionate follower of Jesus.

Kenya – Hospitals Emptied

Here's a powerful example of the influence of children – from Bungoma, Kenya (2004).

Jennifer Toledo writes: *We have been working in Bungoma, Kenya, for four years now and we have seen God demonstrate some of the most amazing miracles through the children time and time again.*

When I first arrived in Bungoma, the churches didn't have much value for the spiritual capacity of children. The children thought they had to wait till they were grown up to 'get saved'. God commissioned me to teach the next generation the 'undiluted gospel'. The majority of the kids I originally worked with were orphans and street kids. But God began to totally transform them with the gospel of the Kingdom, and it wasn't long before everyone everywhere noticed that God was truly with these children.

The Training

To give her children the 'undiluted gospel' as God had said, Jennifer taught her kids about:

    God's plan of redemption
    salvation

being a new creation in Christ
the baptism of the Holy Spirit
the Great Commission

The children spent hours worshipping God, praying, and learning to hear His voice. They memorized verses and passages from the Word of God and applied them to their lives. As a result thousands of children have been equipped and anointed to minister.

In a few months the group had grown to 600 children, from many different churches. Leaders were trained how to help each child use their special gifts from God.

The Kids' Response – Crusades

After this training, the children themselves organized a huge 7-day children's mission. They led open-air crusades and outreaches in fourteen different communities at the same time. Children led the entire outreach. They preached, prophesied, led worship, healed the sick, cast out demons and declared Jesus Christ Lord over their cities.

> "What these children are doing is affecting the whole community."

Every day before the afternoon crusades, the children led a *March for Jesus* through the streets. Businesses everywhere had to stop as the children danced in the streets. On the opening day, 5000 children gathered from many churches. Major government and spiritual leaders, business leaders and teachers, as well as the chief of police gathered to support the children. This was the first time they had all come together like that. Even the head Muslim priest came. "This goes beyond religion," he said. "What these children are doing is affecting the entire community." All these leaders sat and listened while the children preached and shared their hearts, and also pleaded the cause of children at risk. The leaders were touched and pledged to support them.

Casting out demons

The children visited every orphanage in the area, as well as prisons and market places. They did street evangelism, door to door ministry, and ministered in all the hospitals. When they first went into the main hospital, a number of the children had the same vision – a demonic animal was lying on one of the beds. As they prayed the Holy Spirit showed one of the girls it was a spirit of Death that had a stronghold over the hospital. The children immediately began to worship and exalt Jesus because they understood that praise was a powerful weapon against the enemy.[13] As they continued to worship, the demonic animal turned into a woman and ran out of the building. There has not been one death in that hospital for over a year.

Miracles

> *"There were multiple occasions when the children would go into large hospitals, and pray for the sick," Jennifer said, "and we would see entire hospital wards get cleared out. People dying of AIDS, malaria, typhoid, etc. were completely healed, got up out of their beds and went home! Of course all the doctors and nurses got saved witnessing this. One time, the children felt like God wanted them to go to the hospital to pray every day during their lunch break. So out of obedience they went, and sure enough every single day people got miraculously healed. The doctors phoned us a few weeks later and thanked us for sending the children, but told us that we would have to start praying for them because if this kept up they would be without a job. We thought they were joking but over the next several weeks as the children saw healings daily, the hospital was forced to shut down as it could no longer stay in business. People were healed from their diseases before they could be treated by the hospital! We've seen so many miracles!"*

---

13 Ps 8:2

Fasting and Reconciliation

The children met in homes all over the city to pray for the Kingdom of God to come. They called a three month fast to pray for Jesus to change the city. Soon afterwards, two pastors who had been in a legal battle with each other, publicly repented and washed each other's feet. The city pastors, who had been working against each other, came together and repented to the children for not valuing them and giving them their rightful place in the church, and they passed the keys of the city to the children.[14]

Romania – A Boy's Dream Saves a Village

One of today's well-known prophets tells this story from his grandfather. In Grandfather's village in Europe a young boy had a dream. God told him to tell the Christians in the village to leave Romania because severe persecution was coming. The church elders listened to the words of God from the boy. They left Romania and somehow made their way to England. Among them was the prophet's grandfather. Well, we know the story of Romania. Very severe persecution came under Communist rule, and many Christians were imprisoned and killed.

Suppose those elders had not listened. Suppose they were like many church leaders who want to keep the kids in the playroom and give them little stories and colouring books thinking they are not spiritually relevant because they were children.[15]

Maybe the world today would not be hearing one of its most significant prophets.

---

14 From Let the Children by Elizabeth Kotlowski. Jonathan and Jennifer Toledo //www.globalchildrensmovement.com/content/ArchivesItem.phtml?art=12&c=0&id=11&style=
15 Kathy and David Walters, Wind of the Spirit — Urgent Call to Parents and Church Leaders, September 18, 2005 (www.goodnews.netministries.org)

Philippines – A Girl Saves the Church – and Terrorists

She was only 8 years old but God gave her a word for the people at her Church. "God says don't come here next Sunday," she told her congregation. Unlike the congregation in the last story where they listened to God's word from the little boy, no one took any notice of God's word from this little girl. 'God would never say: "Don't come to church"!' they thought.

Next Sunday everyone was there as usual in their thatched pole-house building on the edge of Philippine jungle. But horror! As soon as all had gathered gun-toting guerrillas surrounded them below, yelling and threatening. The little girl walked calmly and stood in the doorway to block their entrance to the meeting hall. The commander yelled up at her to get out of the way, but she just stood there. So he shot her. The bullet went right through her chest and out the other side leaving only a burn mark on her dress. The commander was so rattled he came up the steps at her. He saw that his shot was accurate, but it hadn't harmed her at all. The pastor explained to him that God's power had protected her and His people. The commander recognized that God's power was greater than his and all his soldiers' power despite their fearsome weapons. As a result of the miracle the leader gave his life over to God and his men followed. Everyone was saved that day – the little girl, the congregation and even the terrorists. God had a great victory because one little girl accepted the authority God had given her and spoke powerful words into her jurisdiction – the area over which she had legal right to speak.[16]

India

Many other revivals have started with children. A whole people group, the Naga people, in North East India came to believe and follow Jesus when school kids were touched by the Holy Spirit, and His Kingdom enveloped their whole tribe.

The city of Shillong in Sikkim, India, is a recent example.

---

16 Story told by Dr Garnet Budge, Global Apostolic Network, ca 1983.

You can research these people groups on the web. An inspiring book with lots of stories about how the Holy Spirit loves to use children is: *Let the Children* by Elizabeth Kotlowski.

Another great one was written by Rolland Baker's grandfather about the Holy Spirit visiting children in China, *Visions Beyond the Veil* by HL Baker. It's been republished and God is doing it again, especially with the Bakers in Mozambique.

So be encouraged. You never know how much God will achieve through you when you step up to the plate and start taking charge of your jurisdiction.

~

Chapter 4

Other Jurisdictions And Examples

Of course it goes without saying that the greater the sphere of your influence, the greater your jurisdiction and the greater your potential and responsibility as an agent of change.

Here are some of our early jurisdictional discoveries as we sought to action our new revelations.

Corporations

When I first received this revelation my son-in-law worked for Australia Post. As we discussed the concept of jurisdictions we began to get excited about the extent of his company's jurisdiction. It was responsible for communication to every last address to the very remotest corner of this vast continent – oh, and to the ends of the earth as well! We began to speak into those communication channels reaching every home and business and location in the Nation. We closed doors to evil communications, and opened the channels to good and wholesome stuff and to the Gospel – that every home would be reached by some uncontaminated message from the One Who is the Word (since it's mainly words that create messages and are posted – 'diction').

My son-in-law began to laugh. He had been feeling intimidated by his superiors at work. Now he saw a picture of himself standing like a giant looking down through his toes on the bullies! He realized that he was called to quietly, in the Spirit, unknown to anyone, take charge of the situation in the office. He could disallow the bullying, and speak God's peace, harmony and justice in the workplace. God has called us to reign (we're sons and daughters of the King after all) and He has put our enemies under our feet – not for us to gloat, but so that His kingdom is advanced wherever we are.

Two weeks later I was sharing my new Jurisdictions revelation with a friend who was on the Board of the James Dobson Foundation. I told her of our excitement at the possibility of God's influence over communication channels through Australia Post.

"You won't believe it!" she cried. "Just this week, out of the blue, Australia Post has asked *Focus on the Family* to supply them with enough *How to Drug Proof Your Kids* brochures to make them available at every Post Office in the Nation!" She told me exactly how many there were.

I love it how God does that – gives you a little glimpse of the effect you are having when what you are doing is quite invisible – you're just taking charge of your jurisdiction in the invisible Kingdom, bringing it under God's dominion and influence.

Clinics

Psychologists' clinics are often troubled places; well, troubled people come there for help, and not always of their own volition. I have a friend who works with troubled young people. Sessions sometimes become difficult, even threatening. Dana experimented with her jurisdictional authority. In one particularly difficult session she spoke under her breath to bind an aggressive spirit in the Name of Jesus. To her delight a sudden calm fell over her client.

She decided to take her authority a step further. Why not make her whole area a trouble-free zone? She set a boundary within which Peace and Trust, Hope and Truth ruled. Any attitude conflicting with these was disallowed and must drop off at the door. Each client coming into her office came under her jurisdiction and became the recipient of her Kingdom declarations of God-health, God-will and peace. Then, because these people had come to her for help with their lives she reckoned that their lives, not just her office, fell under her jurisdiction. She began to speak God's love and health over their lives even when they were outside her office, binding and disallowing the operation of the one robbing, killing, or destroying in their lives. She spoke God's principles and His plans over them – His dominion. A parent reported how much happier and 'easier' her son had become.

Building Design

One day I saw a friend's plan for the local Community Centre on public display. My spirit became excited. He draws spaces for people's activities, draws the perimeters and parameters for their movements, the walls that create 'inside' and 'outside' geographically, and the doors between them. Why couldn't he do that spiritually?

We prayed together over the plans of places he had created, particularly public buildings. We disallowed evil and antichrist activities, shut the doors to demonic and political agendas and opened the spaces to good wholesome activities, to God's agendas and plans. We filled the buildings with God's Presence and His attributes, bringing everyone who came into them under His influence. This is the area of my friend's jurisdiction. Those who hire him to draw their plans get ongoing spiritual blessings as a bonus!

Farm Holdings

Meg's son dropped by distressed. He didn't know how he could last in his new job. Although he was team leader he felt helpless to rectify serious problems on the farm and do his job well because of the demands of the section manager. He was distressed for the sick animals and depressed that he could see no solution. Meg suggested that, as a child of God, he take spiritual authority over his work. The farm was under his jurisdiction. He had legal right to speak into the situation – in fact, even over the whole farm. She stood with him as they disallowed current unsavoury practices and spoke health and well-being to stock and staff. They commanded that the atmosphere come into alignment with God's ways, praying that those who refused to conform to His plans for the farm be removed.

He didn't seem very convinced and went off for the weekend still burdened and depressed. On Monday he returned to work to be told that the superior who was causing the problem had resigned and left!

Expect to see that farm blessed and prospering.

Schools

Pat and Sue became concerned when their 12-year-old son's personality began to change. They suspected that drugs were involved and began to investigate. Sure enough they discovered places near the school that children were frequenting to deal and take drugs. Two lots of parents met to take charge of their jurisdiction – this school where their children spent a compulsory part of their lives. They set a spiritual hedge around the property and declared it a safe place for their children. They commanded the drug trafficking in the area to cease, and those involved to become Jesus followers instead. They called in angelic forces to guard the children and to change the atmosphere of the area.

Within a week the vacant house the children had used was totally demolished and removed, and the land turned into a park. The school put up high fences all around their grounds to prevent secret rendezvous with pedlars of evil. A church with a heart for the area rented the school hall for weekend meetings; and *Transformers*[17] set up a parent prayer vigil for the school. In addition the police made some successful drug busts in the area and a meth lab was closed down. The atmosphere is changing.

Postscript: a local drug dealer has given his life to the Lord.

---

17   www.austransformers.com.au Prayer-walking schools for harvest.

Postscript 2: kids from the local area are coming to Pat and Sue's home for times of worship. They pray for each other and give prophetic words. They see visions and discern and cast out spirits. Other kids come to be prayed for, receive Jesus and immediately are able to see in the Spirit realm. Nine kids have been saved over a matter of months. It is all totally spontaneous, happening when it happens!

Gateways

Two couples formed a partnership to buy a piece of land to farm sheep and build themselves homes on a beautiful coastline. It wasn't until later they discovered that God had given them a highly strategic property beside one of the nation's most important lighthouses, giving guidance to ships and aircraft entering the nation. They look across the mouth of the harbour entrance to the capital city. From the lounge window they can watch every ship that enters and exits the harbour and can also see the planes coming in to land at the international airport.

God had called them to be watchmen for the nation. Access in and out of the nation's capital was in their jurisdiction. They began to look at the spiritual responsibility this entailed and to seek God for what they needed to allow and disallow to bring all that busy activity under the Lord's dominion and plan for their nation. They began to form strategies as Gatekeepers for the city and to take their jurisdictional responsibilities seriously. They have drawn a spiritual line across the harbour entrance to the opposite headlands. Illicit trade, contraband, insurrection, endangerment in any way is forbidden to cross that line. They are establishing God's dominion over the Gateway.

Postscript: A visiting prophet recently said of the nation that it was much clearer and lighter than previously. Go the God-appointed watchmen and regents in that nation!

A Beach in Mexico

Cindy Jacobs tells the story of a woman in the US who became burdened in prayer for a particular beach in Mexico. She felt God wanted her to go there. It seemed ridiculous, but she obeyed. Day after day she walked the remote beach praying, asking God what she was there for. Daily there was only one other person on the beach, a lady walking the beach alone. Toward the end of the week they struck up conversation and discovered that each had been told by God to come to this beach and all they knew to do was be obedient and pray. God had brought this particular Mexican beach into their jurisdictions.

They left and returned to their separate homes still not understanding the purpose of the exercise. A week later wild storms crashed onto that coastline and washed out a huge cache of weapons hidden in those cliffs in preparation for an imminent coup!

Your Jurisdiction May Grow

Your jurisdiction may not seem to be very big or important. Work on it and bring it under the Lord's dominion. Let everyone you meet and everything you do be God-influenced. Don't be surprised if your Jurisdiction grows. God has a habit of expanding us, stretching our faith.

Three Dreams

In about '93 God gave me a series of three dreams over a period of three weeks. These dreams became foundations for my understanding of Spiritual Warfare. I later realized that they were showing the growth of my Jurisdiction, the progression of my spheres of influence.

Dream 1

> My home was a large open-plan house and a neighbour kept coming in and taking things. At first I paid little attention. Nice that he was comfortable to make himself at home – one of the family. But as it went on I began to feel indignant. This wasn't right. He should ask, not just come and help himself to my things. Then one day I found him carrying out my TV. I began to politely protest that, if he wanted to borrow things, he should ask first. He took no notice

of me, so I told him, "No, you can't have it." He still ignored me and kept walking out with it. So I said more firmly, "NO! You can't have it." When he still took no notice, I repeated it more loudly and, to get his attention, I hit him on the head with a cardboard cylinder I was holding. I was determined now! No, he could not just take my things. I kept bopping him on the head with my cardboard cylinder stating that he was not to take my things. He eventually backed out the door leaving the TV behind. Then I felt terrible! Fancy hitting the neighbour on the head! I was afraid he might gather some cronies and come back in revenge.

Dream 2

I was in what appeared to be a hired hall with people who were running a meeting there. I didn't know them, but they were telling me about the marauders who would come and break in, damage their property and intimidate and harass them. As they were talking, we saw men passing the side window. "Here they are!" the people cried out and all cowered in behind me. I found myself standing in front of these believers facing the door where the thugs were about to enter. "No, you can't come in!" I said approaching the doorway, standing to my full 4 feet 10 inches and expanding myself to try and fill the doorway. "No, you can't come in!" I said with greater determination and, would you know, the cardboard cylinder was in my hand again. "Get out! Get out!" I was saying, whacking with my cardboard cylinder until they all fell back and disappeared into the dark. I was amazed. Those burly fellows could have knocked me over with a feather!

Interpretations

I realized that these dreams were both about spiritual warfare and God was growing my understanding:

    1. I had to recognize Satan for what he was and be aware of what

he was doing. He comes to rob.
2. I had to learn to say "no" and not just allow things to go on, or myself to be robbed.
3. I had to be absolutely determined against Satan, no polite platitudes, no neighbourly concessions or excuses. Don't LET him get away with things.
4. The cylinder held the certificate of my Power of Attorney on God's behalf. I was wielding my God-given authority, acting on His behalf and with His legal backing.
5. I need not be intimidated by the enemy and afraid of 'backlash'. My fear allowed him to get away with things. His activity stopped when I stood up to him. He didn't come back; it was a lying thought, invoking fear. Resist the devil and he will flee from you. (Jas 4:7).
6. I had a spiritual authority that intimidated the enemy. The power I had was nothing to do with my own size or strength.
7. I had authority to act not only on my own behalf, but had a calling to act on behalf of God's ecclesia (called out people) and protect them. I could stand in the gap for them and also demonstrate for them how to resist.

Dream 3

I was on the outskirts of a village, a cluster of thatched roundhouses I took to be possibly in Africa. Some of the villagers had come out and were gathered around me distressed about the wild animals that kept coming and destroying their crops, taking their domestic animals and endangering their lives. As they were talking several animals appeared out of the bush and began approaching us. They looked like a cross between large pigs and bears. I waved my arms and shouted at them, "Shoo, get off!" When they were a bit slow and reluctant to go I set out aggressively at them shooing them away. Most ran off back into the jungle, but one kept coming towards me

– and I to it. How dare he! I grabbed it around the head, forcing its mouth shut and pressing it tightly into my stomach. It was a big solid animal. I was trying to twist and break its neck to drop the beast, but it was too big and heavy for me. All my strength and weight couldn't do it. I knew if I let go it would gore me. So I was stuck there holding on to it, saying to the villagers, "You're going to have to kill it". I had captured it, they needed to deal with and put an end to it, and fast – without killing me in the process!

This last dream showed an expansion of my jurisdiction from the Church to Nations. But this last devil I couldn't drive off on my own. It needed the aggressive involvement of the local people. I could capture the beast for them. I had God-given authority to oppose the attacker they had come to me about. But they themselves had to be involved, take some responsibility. I couldn't do it alone, but I had to hold on and not give up until they rose to the challenge.

I also realized how faith begets faith. Those harassed by the enemy need to see faith in action to be encouraged to rise up themselves and resist the enemy.

So I learned that my Jurisdiction began at home, and, as my faith grew, it expanded to the Church, and then to the Nations.

The next chapter will demonstrate some jurisdictional initiatives that definitely grew me.

~

Chapter 5
Who Is In Charge Here?

Protestors, Police or God?

One day God shook me to my core. I'd just attended a national prayer event at Uluru (Ayers Rock), Central Australia. Along with Aboriginal leaders from numbers of tribes we were 'reclaiming the land' and dedicating it to its true Owner, the Lord. (*The earth is the Lord's...* Ps. 24:1) Back home, I opened the local newspaper and the headline daggered my heart: **Developer Reclaims Land,** it blared.

I felt God saying, "So you've been off to Uluru, 'reclaiming land'. What about your own backyard? I put you here with spiritual authority in this town; what are you doing about it?"

For almost two years my little town had been waging a mini civil war. Some of our residents were strongly opposed to a multinational supermarket coming to town. They fought fiercely. Protestors were bussed in; marches and demonstrations disrupted 'business as usual'; a 'platypus embassy' arose on the site, and someone lived in a tree there for months (until he fell out and broke a leg).

The police had to establish a continuous presence to both protect the site and maintain peace in the town. Even mounted police were called in on occasion to quell the violence and restore order in our main street. All the strife even made international headlines!

Now God was saying, "This is your jurisdiction, Joye, and you're allowing all this chaos and lawlessness!" I was mortified. I hadn't seen it like that before!

The following Sunday afternoon, after our collective worship, I led the group to a place where we could overlook the site. (I thought better of asking permission to actually go on site; it would be too politically messy.) So from across the stream we worshipped, read scripture and made proclamations. I didn't know what God's perspective on multinationals was (did He care?), but we took responsibility for the violence, the division and the lawlessness in our community, and asked forgiveness. We bound those spirits in Jesus' Name and declared Peace over our town and the site. We took authority in the Spirit realm and **shut down demonic agendas, political agendas and man's agendas, and locked the situation into God's agendas.**

After everyone left I walked down to the road and stood on the bridge, gazing up the stream that bordered the site. A policeman left his car and came over. "Ok God, you do want them to know about this."

"Thank you for all you're doing for the town," I smiled. "A group of us from different churches have just been thanking God for you and praying for the site, asking for peace in the town, praying against the lawlessness."

He shuffled his shiny boots, cleared his throat, and talked about the weather.

Two days later the police presence was withdrawn. There has not been another march, demonstration or protest. In three months the supermarket was built and running (and visitors remark on the lovely atmosphere of peace in the shop!).

I was stunned! "Lord," I said, "I didn't know I had so much power. This is a huge responsibility!"

All this is to say: You have the power to change the atmosphere around you. Recognize your jurisdiction and the extent of it and take the authority God has assigned you over it. Be careful to stay within the borders of what God has allocated to you. However know that, if God has allocated it into your jurisdiction, He has given you the authority, the resources and the protection to bring about His purposes.

Here's another story about Who's in charge:

Witches, Warlocks or God?

My home town is (geographically!) high and there's a high place outside of town. Some sensitive people have found the town spooky and avoided coming here. Incense filled the air, yellow-robed people strolled the street along with dread-locked young people sitting about. Signs read, 'Experience the magic'.

It was nearing midnight one night in the early days of my residence in the town when a pastor rang me. "Joye, it's satanic new year and there are bonfires on the high place opposite you. Just letting you know to be in prayer." I went to my piano and began to worship. That's my kind of warfare, taken straight out of Psalm 149. *'Jesus Your Name is above every other'*... I was having a good time. I was in the middle of singing *'Nothing is impossible ...'* when there was a loud crack like a rifle shot inside the piano. I swung my legs away, but continued playing and singing. I wasn't going to be stopped making this declaration of God's greatness. Nothing seemed wrong with the piano, no broken strings. I kept on worshipping for a while, then went off to bed.

I must have been asleep about half an hour when once again there was the sound of a rifle shot, right beside my head. To my surprise I snuggled down into the blankets and heard myself say, "You can't intimidate me, Satan". I had a sound sleep with no further disturbance.

Oddly enough, several days later I discovered a gnome (which sat on a pedestal in the rainforest of my rented home) was on his face in the dirt. More surprising still, his face was at the base of the pedestal and his feet away from it. He could not have naturally fallen to that position. I had only discovered him a few weeks earlier and with a missionary friend we decided, since neither the gnome nor the property belonged to me, there was nothing

I could physically do with it. So we prayed that anything untoward in it would bow to God's dominion and have no influence on the property.

I rang the missionary. "Did you dethrone the gnome?"

"No," he answered, "I never returned there".

I asked the guy who did the lawns. "No."

"Hmm!" I said. "Ok Lord, I know now what you think about gnomes!" I believe God felled that Dagon in a clash of powers on the night of the satanic new year.[18]

Our group felt to visit the high place where the occultists met. Pastor had discovered that there were six leylines[19] intersecting on that point, facilitating occult communication across the area. We believed God wanted us to go therefore we had His authority to do so. We had additional authority in the spirit realm because one of our number was an ex-witch. In training as a high-priestess she had actually astral travelled and taken part in satanic rituals here. A group of us accessed the place (on foot) and our first act was Repentance. The ex-witch repented on behalf of all the idolatrous wickedness and ceremonies which had taken place there. (Repentance is the base-line for all spiritual warfare.) We found a car wheel formed into a cauldron for blood sacrifice. We repented of the blood sacrifices and cleansed the land with the Blood of Jesus (symbolically using wine). We demolished pentagonal altars in the Name of Jesus throwing the rocks down the mountainside, cleansed the land, and in the process uncovered cremated human remains guarded by an unusual snake which the pastor, like Moses, took up by the tail and killed in Jesus' Name.

Then we began to cut the leylines. The ex-priestess repented of the astral travel which she had been involved in along those lines. Our silk banners dropped suddenly as we spiritually cut the first line. Then they picked up and fluttered in another direction. When we prayed for the leyline in that direction and cut it in the spirit realm, the banners suddenly dropped again. Each time, after a moment, they picked up and fluttered

---

18   1 Sam 5

19   Leylines: communication lines in the occult spirit world. They link places of occult significance and provide spirit highways used in astral travel. Where the lines cross are significant power points.

in another direction, so we followed the wind believing it was the wind of the Holy Spirit literally giving us direction. Each time as the line severed the silk banners dropped. This was a most encouraging sign to us.

A couple of years later a local pastor called me, excited. A history buff, he had done a lot of research in the area and written on its history. Someone approached him at the Historical Society's Show and asked him for a copy of a page he had on display. "What interests you?" he'd queried.

"You say that the name of our stream means 'mischievous spirits,'" she said. "We have been trying for two years to research why our leylines are blocked."

He asked if she knew me, which she didn't, then if she was a Christian. "Oh no," she said. "We far predate Christianity."

'From the horse's mouth!' I was elated. What we do in the spirit realm is sheerly by faith and rarely by sight. But every now and then the Lord lifts the veil and lets us see what is being accomplished. I love Him for it! I felt like Gideon outside the tent listening to the enemy tell his dream of the little barley loaf that would wipe them out – expressing their fear that Gideon's little band was about to defeat them in battle.[20]

Once, the witches and warlocks were in charge here. Now no longer. The high place is clear, the atmosphere is fresh, the population is changing. We heard later that a proposed world gathering of witches and warlocks was unable to access these hills.

Death and Violence, or God

"Murder Capital" the headlines shouted. The city had been my home for some years in the past. We had prayer-walked and taken territory. In the governmental arena civic leaders were asking our advice and were prepared to support our suggestions. There was a recognition that civic and spiritual leaders needed to work side by side to solve societal problems.

Now, some years down the track, Satan was making this declaration. How dare he! We are the Spiritual Custodians of our societies – the

---

20 Judges 7

caretakers of the spirit realm over our cities. We were responsible to make sure this curse declared over our city did not 'take'.

> We are the Spiritual Custodians of our communities – the caretakers of the spirit realm over our cities.

Praying people got together and first defined the boundaries. We drove around the perimeter of the city, as many had done before, and declared that this specific area was to come under the Lord's dominion of peace. Within these boundaries we were making war on the spiritual strongman, Violence; identifying this enemy and his associates[21] (murder, suicide, self-harm, abuse, intimidation, etc.). *'Satan comes to rob, to kill and destroy, but Jesus came to destroy the works of the devil.'* (Jn 10:10)

We mobilized prayer and care for victims, and for organizations working with violence and its effects. After a time of city-wide consultation, prayer and building of faith we held a 'battle' to which all churches, Christian and civic leaders and pray-ers were invited.

The 'battle' was held in a park beside the Council Chambers and consisted of three parts, Repentance, Binding, Blessing, ending with Thanksgiving and Worship.

Worship preceded each segment and a different minister led prayers in each part before a collective prayer was read. Room was made for spontaneous contributions from those present under each of the above headings. Significant prophecies from the past were read in the last segment and a respected prophetess declared over the city.

The battle ended with worship and a Prophetic Act. An imaginary meandering line became the Jordan River. On one side was the Wilderness; on the other side the Promised Land. Everyone stepped across the river into the 'Promised Land'.

God said, "Today leave the wilderness behind; leave the slavery

---

21 See Josh 13:21 Moses defeated King Sihon and all the princes allied with him.

and poverty, the violence and murder behind. Today you have stepped across the Jordan into the Promised Land – the land of His Promises to you. Jericho, the first city, has been taken. There are many others, but God is with you to take the whole land and bring it under His dominion.

"There is a remarkable spring in the city Jericho, in Israel. In the time of Elisha the people complained to the prophet that its water was brackish and undrinkable. Prophets have solutions. "Put salt in it," he said. (He didn't give a recipe, saying how much, it was just the obedience.) From that day the waters were cleansed and today thousands of gallons of the purest water pour out of that artesian spring, supplying the city of Jericho and its surrounds. There's a plaque there telling the story and giving God glory. But God is saying today that in this city He has opened a well, a spring of the purest water where even the shyest of creatures can come and drink – it's a spring of pure living water that will bring cleansing and healing to everyone who comes, and people will come from far and near to drink of this purity."

The statistical results in our target city show murders have visibly decreased. The Mayor called a week-long forum with all interested parties, and the community was asked to suggest and engage in positive remedies. The atmosphere of the city has changed and civic and Christian leaders are working together creatively to address the roots as well as the manifestations of violence in the city.

And it's true, people are coming internationally to drink of springs of living water, revelation and refreshing in the city.

Siva, Destruction or God?

A thousand years ago King Jayavarman 11 of the great Kampuchean Empire (Cambodia) dedicated his Nation to the Hindu god, Siva, god of Destruction. From that day on the reigning Emperor annually renewed the contract and Cambodia knew nothing but Destruction. It hit me as I landed in the capital's derelict airport in 1991 on a six week assignment with *World Vision*.

> The cadavers of once-mighty helicopters eye us helplessly from the sidelines like limp, morteined mosquitoes. There's something tragic about their emasculation. Signs of destruction are everywhere. It shouts at you wherever you look. Destruction for the sake of destruction – the lovely bridge spanning the Mekong just a bomb-severed arm reaching desperately into space, its chunk of access freeway lying overgrown and chewed by goats. Temples have been pulled stone from stone and strewn across the fields. Cities emptied and left to ruin, their occupants driven like slaves to hard labour in the distant countryside. Phnom Penh was an elegant French colonial city – gracious homes flanking wide tree-lined boulevards … It took only four short years for one madman to destroy a nation – wipe out everything … perhaps three million lives. My mind trembles at the thought.[22]

The day before I left on this assignment, my home congregation gathered about me to pray. Spontaneous prayer burst forth. Something was happening to the people and I stood in the centre of it. Afterwards people were grabbing me, tears streaming, some in great excitement. A woman kept saying, "I was so amazed!" "Amazed at what?" I asked bewildered. "At the power that was there," she said. I had no idea about jurisdictions then, but God was setting something up.

Cambodia felt like home; I had lived for many years in Indonesia and it felt similar to old Java in some ways. It enfolded me and poured its stories into me. Interesting extra-curricular assignments cropped up not organized by man. Miraculously I was permitted to explore King Sihanouk's palace as workmen prepared it for his imminent return from exile. An unseen King came with me and prepared the palace spiritually as

---

[22] JA. 'Glimpses', Journey Writers, Peranga Post Publishers, 2003.

well! Then, around the corner I stopped the cyclo[23] driver and prophesied over a sound shell. "From this place crowds will listen to the Gospel."[24] (The country was still under Vietnam's Communist rule at the time.)

I had no idea that throughout the assignment God was establishing my jurisdiction in this nation. He was also preparing others. In 1995 He pulled together a convergence of people with jurisdiction – people He was giving the legal right to speak over this nation.

> The land is drenched with the blood of its people down the centuries. If this land is to be healed and the Gospel bring its restoring power, then the ruling prince of the kingdom of darkness must be deposed.[25]

Here is team leader John Robb's report[26] of what happened:

> *Approximately 50 Christian leaders from a number of churches and organizations (there were only 9 churches when I was there in '91) gathered in Phnom Penh for a three-day conference on strategic-level intercession. There were 11 on our international team from seven nationalities representing the Body of Christ around the world. As we listened to prayer concerns from this traumatized society, God brought to the surface the need for people present to repent of their participation in violence during the Pol Pot times. A dike of emotion broke and there was public confession of heinous crimes which conference participants had themselves committed.*

Assessing the authority we had – Kjell Sjoberg:
1. *This repentance of blood guilt gave us the primary authority.*
2. *The scriptures the Lord had given – 'rhema' words for this*

---

23   Cyclo – an Indochina pedicab, like a pushchair driven by an elevated cyclist.
24   This was the exact location where Cambodia's part in the Global March for Jesus (1994) ended with a Gospel Rally.
25   JA War in Cambodia, 'Intercessor', March 1995.
26   World Vision International Memo, March 23, 1995. Used by permission.

occasion.
3. *Leaders from all over the country – a truly national representation.*
4. *The transdenominational representation of the Body of Christ.*
5. *A truly international team – representing the global Body of Christ.*
6. *The enormous prayer backing from across the world – more than had ever been known until then.*

We took communion, then spent a day praying in teams at locations which the Khmer people selected as strategic. (This was with solemn warning that if anyone still had unconfessed sin to please not participate; this would jeopardise both themselves and the team.) *The following day the international team accompanied five godly Cambodian leaders to Angkor Wat, the largest religious structure in the world – an astronomical sun-worshiping temple, originally Hindu, but now Buddhist. Every labourer to ever work on constructing the site became a human sacrifice; no labourer ever left the site.*

We supported our Cambodian brothers as they repented of the bloodshed and idolatry and proclaimed Jesus King of Kings. With trembling and tears they put a lid on the gaping hole of the bottomless pit. They sealed the gates to the dissemination of darkness and declared the gates open to the King of Glory.[27] *They also severed the occult connection of the Khmer Rouge to these temples so they could no longer draw power from this unholy place and continue to wreak death in the countryside.*

Mount Bakheng was our last location. This is where the King made his pact with Siva. From here we could see the temple (at the time under Khmer control) where his annual sex rituals with the Naga were carried out to renew the contract. The Khmer leaders, the spiritual kings,[28] led in a ceremony to revoke this covenant on behalf of their Nation and established instead a contract with the living God. The international

---

27 Ps 24
28 Rev 1:6; 5:10

team stood alongside them as they did this; it was a Khmer contract. The brothers poured their water over a map of Cambodia symbolizing cleansing and life where once the waters carried blood and the seed of the Naga. I loved that local children joined in holding out their hands towards the map as we pronounced the land under Jesus' dominion.

Then a cobra skin was laid out and we symbolically trod upon the defeated serpent. To me that was a most powerful moment. When I stepped onto that snake I began to jump and laugh. I knew the power of the Naga had been defeated and his hold broken, not only in Cambodia, but wherever his influence had flowed from here – down to Bali, and on.

Today Cambodia is a transformed nation. The Gospel is freely proclaimed, Jesus is known and worshipped, churches have been established across the land. Revival has broken out in several communities. The Khmer Rouge have been brought to justice and stable government instituted by the people. Cambodia is a hive of Christian workers and activities busily building an eternal kingdom, not subject to a mortal god-king or ruled by death and destruction, but responding to the Life and Light of the King of Kings.

The Holy Spirit, the great heavenly conductor, orchestrated this transformation. Jurisdictions converged and overlapped as the Body of Christ flowed together, each part honouring the others' gifts, each taking responsibility for the role assigned them.

It may not be a city or a nation, but you do have a jurisdiction for which you are responsible and in which you can make an atmospheric difference and bring heaven to earth. You have the power to change the atmosphere where God places you.

You, God's regent, are the one appointed to take charge of the jurisdiction he has given you.

~

Chapter 6
Who Is In Charge Here –
Baal or Yahweh?

Bali Bomb, 2005 Christmas letter

One night in 2005 I received a phone call from Bali. "Bu, pray! Bombs have gone off just around the corner. Alicia's going to help in the hospital." My daughter and son-in-law live in Jimbaran, the latest suburb to be terror-targeted. It was their wedding anniversary and friends had taken the children the night before and sent the parents off for a night, otherwise they might have celebrated at that restaurant. Alicia spent an amazing night assessing who should be medevac'd out – translating for doctors and patients, bringing calm and professionalism in the midst of the trauma and chaos. A lesson to me was: God didn't have to boom out of Heaven, "Don't go to that restaurant!" It was just in the ordinary everyday decisions of righteous people. 'The steps of a good man are ordered by the Lord.'

A week later the Lord spoke unexpectedly: "I gave you Bali, what are you doing about it?" Suddenly it wasn't just a pretty phrase saying 'we rule and reign with Christ'! There was a huge responsibility involved.

Since then He has been downloading to me about our responsibility.

We have an inheritance to occupy – actually the Lord's inheritance, so if we don't occupy it He doesn't get His inheritance. We have all the resources and authority necessary to dislodge the illegal occupants/trespassers. This is not just an invitation, it's a responsibility. God is calling us to reclaim our families, our cities, and our nations. We live and walk in a spirit world unlimited by time and place, and we are inhabited by the Holy Spirit.

At this stage I had no understanding of Jurisdictions, but the Lord was laying ground work.

Ten years earlier, while on the Prayer Initiative in Cambodia (1995) I sensed a link between Cambodia and Bali. I had come to believe that Bali's ruling strongman was Siva, the same entity King Jayavarman II had sold his nation to. There were all sorts of similarities – looks, language, engravings, temples, culture and, yes, the spiritual 'ruling party' – all reminded me of my Bali years. I found the old Balinese felt that in an unspecific past, they were linked ancestrally with Cambodia. Both Cambodia and Bali had been part of extensive Hindu Empires at differing times – Kampuchean (9th – 15th centuries) and Majapahit (1293-1520). Each nation was controlled by the strongman Siva and each was discerned by intercessors to be a seat of Satan.

I sensed too an ancient link between Bali and Baal – manifested in Israel's history as the golden calf diverting their worship from the true God. In Hinduism the cow is sacred, and in Bali the dead are placed in the effigy of a bull to be cremated and purified for *Nirvana*. Siva's vehicle is a sacred bull symbolizing might. In Canaanite lore, Baal was the ruler of Heaven as well as god of the sun, rain, thunder, fertility, and agriculture. Also known as 'Rider of the Clouds', 'Almighty', and 'Lord of the Earth', he is the most aggressive of the gods. Bali's goddess of the lake (Dewi Danau), is arguably a manifestation of Astarte/Ishtar, consort of Baal. She is in charge of sacred pools and water, and Baal is associated with an agricultural system by which the rain drains down to bring fertility to the fields. (The Balinese are famous for their ingenious ancient irrigation [subak] systems feeding the island's rice fields.) Interestingly, some Celts hold that their god, Belenos of the sun and springs of water has links with Baal. The root Bal means strong, mighty, hence 'Baal the greater god', or in Hebrew 'owner' or 'master/lord'. Britannica explains that Babylonians pronounced it Bel, which ultimately became the Greek Belos, identified with Zeus. In the original Sanskrit and in Balinese balin means warrior. (I believe this to be one of the Redemptive giftings of the Balinese.) So it would seem that definitions of Siva and Baal overlap.

All these interchanging, inter-relating gods seem very confusing to western minds. Remember that these are spirit rulers. The myths and legends of different communities seek to explain, and in the case of Bali engage, the obvious spirit world around them. Often the same spirit manifests in different forms or under different names in different cultures. Their character however remains the same, and even they are 'known by their works'. Their aim is always to rob, kill, destroy and to divert all worship from the true God.

At the collapse of the Majapahit Empire (that extended from Java perhaps as far as the Mekong River) a large number of courtiers, artisans, priests, and members of Javanese royalty moved east to the island of Bali.[29] Bali
    resisted the advance of Islam as it marched through the archipelago,
    resisted Dutch colonization until the early 1900's, and
    resisted Christianity.

It had remained an impregnable stronghold for centuries and the Gospel had made little headway.

I asked the leader of our Cambodian team, John Robb, if he would consider a similar initiative in Bali to the one we had just completed in Cambodia. The result was that almost the identical team came to Bali the following year.

Here are extracts from John's report (italics) along with my observations.

---

29 http://www.allempires.com/forum/forum_posts.asp?TID=3982

BALI PRAYER INITIATIVE CASE STUDY: 1996
John D. Robb[30]
Introduction

Bali is one of the most beautiful places on earth. A favorite tourist destination it offers towering mountains, magnificent beaches, perfect surfing, and fascinating cultural events. Balinese are gentle, polite people extremely gifted in art, music and dance. Yet, unless they are spiritually perceptive, there is a dark side to Bali most tourists never see. My parents and other visiting Christians described spiritual oppression like an iron band around their heads. A long-term missionary to Bali participated in the Cambodia prayer initiative. With local Christian leaders she invited our team to do a similar initiative there in July 1996.

I began to research the island's history, culture, religious beliefs, and status of Christianity leading up to this special prayer effort. I was looking for basically two things:

1. *The identity of the spiritual strongman. Bali is known as Pulau Dewata, 'the isle of the gods'. There are many gods, demons and ancestral spirits worshiped, but which one is the chief honcho, the one Jesus would describe in Mark 3:27 as the main power holding the island and its people captive?*
2. *How does the spiritual strongman maintain its control, for this is the essence of the demonic, the attempt to control and dominate human beings and their institutions.*

In this research effort, my missionary friend supplied some good material, and I did a lot of study at a university library. During our visit to Bali, I also interviewed local Christian workers and two Hindu priests, one of whom had converted

---

30 Used by permission.

to Christ. I want to share the picture which emerged from this research process and how it helped to guide our prayer initiative, as well as to report on what God did.

Bali is a solitary Hindu outpost amidst the thousands of predominantly Muslim islands of the Indonesian archipelago. Before the coming of Hinduism ancient Indonesians worshiped nature gods – god of the sun, mountains, sea – as well as invoking the souls of the ancestors. Even today Balinese believe the abode of the Gods is on the mountains, and rocks, trees, winds, birds, streams, and lakes are inhabited by multitudes of local place spirits which are the owners of these objects and are said to become touchy unless properly placated. (To the Balinese literally everything, visible and invisible is ranked, ordered and identified according to location. 'Kaja' towards the mountains, the gods, and good. 'Kelod' towards the sea, earthly, ominous, demonic.) **Bali belongs to the gods**, they say. The island's inhabitants are only transitory tenants, with the gods the true owners of the land. People still also pray to the spirits of their ancestors as sustainers of their lives.

(The gods created Bali as a flat, barren place. But when neighbouring Java fell to the Muslims, the disgusted Hindu gods moved to Bali and, at each of the four cardinal points, built mountains high enough for their exalted rank. In the middle they created the volcano Gunung Agung (Great Mountain), also called the 'Cosmic Mountain' and 'Navel of the World'.)[31]

Hinduism, and Buddhism came to Java and Bali in the fifth century, melding a mishmash of old beliefs into a convenient syncretism. All the gods overcrowding the Balinese pantheon, including Brahma and Vishnu, who form with Shiva a Hindu trinity, came eventually to be considered manifestations of

---

31 www.angelfire.com/nt2/oz2002indo/story/turtle.htm

Shiva[32]. (This philosophy neatly complied with Government demand after the communist coup of 1965 that every citizen adhere to a monotheistic religion. It is now held that above the plethora of gods Sang Hyang Widi Wasa is the originator of everything and manifests in all these other ways.)

The chief shrines in the temples are to Shiva, and his consort or female half, Durga or Rangda, goddess of death and destruction. The joint male/ female component runs through the whole culture. Rangda represents indestructible fear, also black magic, witchcraft and especially love magic. There is a strong sexual character to Bali Hinduism, the phallic pillars (seen also throughout Indo-china) are a symbol of Siva. Witchcraft is fought by the use of white magic personified by Barong, in the famous dance depicting the struggle between good and evil.

(The main lesson of the Barong dance is that evil to Balinese thinking is indestructible and cannot be ultimately overcome. It can only be kept within certain limits if successfully placated by acceptable rituals and offerings.)

Pious Balinese housewives make offerings three times a day (otherwise the spirits may steal the food from their children's plates). *Shiva is the one who gives occult power, and sorcerers obtain from him the ability to transform themselves into spirits in animal form. On Bali, sorcerers hold spirit battles to the death.*

The above material was readily uncovered through documentary study and the identity of the spiritual strongman as Shiva/ Surya was later confirmed to me in interviews with local Christian leaders.

Strongholds, in my opinion, are places where the strongman (Mark 3:27) grips a people group in order to maintain his control. Three ways he does this in Bali are through

1. *fear-inspired worship rites*
2. *the shedding of blood*
3. *lines of occult power*

---

32 In Bali known as 'Siva.'

An international team of ten prayer leaders and intercessors from five nations joined 70 local Christian workers from the island of Bali and other Indonesian islands for a prayer initiative organized by the Indonesia Evangelical Fellowship.

This wasn't some insignificant little exercise someone thought up. What was so awesome is that God had it planned from the foundation of the earth, and 30 years earlier He was already weaving my destiny in with this island and establishing my jurisdiction here, laying groundwork for this pivotal event.

There were possibly one million intercessors praying for this venture.
* Yonggi Cho sent a personal letter: his congregation and those on Prayer Mountain were praying.
* The Prayer Warriors in Solomon Islands prayed 24hours a day on their Prayer Mountain and studied Bali in a special Unreached People's Group Module the week before.
* Intercessors for the Philippines faxed to say their National Network was concentrating on Bali over that week.
* Peter Wagner's network was engaged – 40 prayer organizations attached to the AD2000 and Beyond Movement.
* *PrayerLink* readers were alerted throughout the Pacific.
* 340 churches in Sri Lanka, plus hundreds of other prayer warriors in Scandinavia, Singapore, Cambodia, Australia, the United States and more.

After a night's sleep the first activity of the team was an orientation tour including a trance dance (with their prior approval). To my surprise, I was the one affected by this drama although I had seen it before. When a goddess offered her son as a sacrifice to the Rangda I was in agonies. He was beaten and tied to a tree. It was me being sacrificed! It was so strong I began to rebuke the 'spirit of sacrifice'. The prince rose to life again and drove off the Rangda and I felt happy. Then in the finale, when the men run in and stab themselves and the priest comes sprinkling holy water and brings them out of the trance, I began weeping. I tried to control it, but when we reached the car park, I was overcome again, weeping with deep intercession and grief. The team, gathering around me to pray, recognized that I had been carrying a microcosm of what was going on in Bali – that in a sense I was standing in for Bali.

We journeyed on and I suddenly caught sight of a brick wall standing alone like a fake movie set along the edge of a rice field. On it was graffitied ONESTONE.

Here is John's account: *On the first morning, as our team ate breakfast together at an outdoor restaurant overlooking the sea, Mt Agung visible in the distance, we felt God was giving us a strategy. Two of us had been meditating on the same scripture, David's battle with Goliath. A prayer leader from California had given me the same passage before departure. 'It only took one stone.' God guided that stone to its mark as David moved forward in simple faith, refusing to be deterred by the curses and threats of the monster enemy. We felt the Lord was telling us to keep focused on Him and He would guide all our prayers to become the knockout blow Shiva deserved.*

Later that day as our minibus took us into the mountains, someone cried, "Stop. Did you see what was written on that wall?" The driver backed up obligingly and we clambered out to have a look. There on the wall, painted in large white English letters was: It only takes one stone to crumble the loser.

The Lord's strategy for this trip was the strategic, accurate placement of David's one stone. We took a photo of this bizarre sign – one weird wall in a rice field with no seeming purpose other than to speak to us. One stone would certainly fell the façade.

The scripture the Lord had given me prior to coming was:
>Shall the prey be taken from the mighty or the lawful captive delivered? But so says the Lord: "Even the captives of the mighty shall be taken away and the prey of the fearsome ones shall escape. For I will contend with him who contends with

you and I will save your children." Is 49:24

John Robb continues:

THE SEMINAR ran Monday and Tuesday with around 70 pastors and intercessors attending. (Disappointingly, only a minority of these were ethnic Balinese. Most churches are led and attended by non-Balinese.)
Local Christian leaders briefed us on the obstacles they face:
* *The extreme bondage of religious custom and tradition*
* *The tight-knit social structure in which the people had no concept of making a decision apart from the community (no individual identity)*
* *Government intransigence in approving permits to build churches (nine official agreements needed)*
* *Persecution by government and community leaders*
* *The bishop of the Protestant church said, "The most important thing is to pray that the Balinese will be able to conquer the evil spirit. They are even afraid to sleep alone at night."*
* *Added to that are internal problems of lack of cooperation, sheep stealing, and conflict between Christian leaders. Of course, with disunity, united prayer efforts are difficult to bring off.*

Local ministers and team members (John Robb, Kjell Sjoberg and Leslie Keegel) brought teaching interspersed with times of united intercession for unreached subgroups of the society, and needs of churches and parachurch organizations.
Kjell Sjoberg, *our loved Swedish leader, revealed that: The National sin of Bali is worshipping the creation instead of the Creator. Never in the 83 countries I have visited have I seen so much worship of the creation. God has created Bali to reveal His own personality and purpose* (Bali's Redemptive Purpose). *Satan wants to block God's voice in creation. He has done this most effectively since the whole island has been sacrificed to the gods... But*

spiritual strongholds are no problem for a united church. Therefore the groundwork before spiritual warfare always involves reconciliation in the Body of Christ. He spoke about the power of the blood of Jesus to bring healing to the land and reconciliation in the Body of Christ.

Identificational repentance was a new concept, but a Balinese brother broke out with a prayer of repentance on behalf of his people for worshipping false gods. Others followed repenting of sun-worship, idolatry and ancestral worship. A Dutchman asked forgiveness for invading their land and the bloody massacres that ensued. Amazingly a Balinese princess was present, descendant of the king of Badung who with his people fell on their swords in a ceremonial mass suicide (*puputan*) at the invasion. She stepped up to express forgiveness. One who had lost many of his family in the 1965 blood bath expressed forgiveness to a brother repenting on behalf of the Balinese for murdering their own people. Blood guilt was dealt with.[33] They also repented deeply for worshipping creation rather than the Creator.

Prayer Excursions were made on the third day to the most significant temples.
1. **Besaki** (meaning dragon), the mother temple, located on Mt Agung, home of Siva. There the Balinese pastors, supported by the rest of us, broke the covenant with Siva, god of destruction and spiritual strongman of the island. They wept in repentance and intercession for their people. Then they made a new covenant with the Living God. The Balinese entered the temple supported by the men from our team, while we 40 others circumnavigated this huge structure – first in repentance for the worship and sacrifice to false gods, and a second time making declarations from the Word.

    This major action was followed by visits to other significant sites of spiritual darkness and control, including massacre sites.

---

33 Is 26:2-27:1

2. **Mt Batur and the Crater Lake.** This is my territory. I spent my second term in Bali (1967-69) trekking this crater (reportedly the largest active crater in the world. The active cone is inside the crater flanked by a large lake.) I searched out every village I could find hidden away in those inaccessible mountain fastnesses. There I told them the story of Jesus for the first time. Clambering these mountain trails on foot, singing, or weeping and interceding, my tears dripping into the dirt paths, I never dreamed that this was the habitation of the major stronghold on the island, and residence of the most powerful priest. Nor had I any idea that my circuit of villages formed the power hub of the Goddess of the Lake. Dewi Danau, consort of Siva, controlled the life-giving water resources which make Bali so lush and productive. Since she controlled the water systems, to her all the people come for holy water, which is then used across the island in all their ceremonies. She is the one who, more than any other, demands human sacrifice – including annually into the lake. Although this is now replaced with the living sacrifice of a buffalo "she will take a human sacrifice within six months".

We prayed at her temple, as before the Balinese going in and revoking the contracts, and the rest of us walking around the outside first repenting then making scriptural proclamations.

A song began to tumble out of me and only as we sang did we realize what a prophetic declaration it was. *"Jesus, redemption's sacrifice..." His Kingdom,* by Darlene Czech. Look it up and marvel at the aptness of the prophetic word for the situation.

From here we spilt into groups and went to various places. John was eager to meet

3. **The Jero Gede,** the Siva High Priest at the Crater Lake, of whom he had read in his research. On Sunday the Jero's wife had made an appointment with us to meet him down by the Lake today.

This was an amazing meeting. He was not the priest I had known formerly, but I had spoken with him on occasion when I lived here. It was John's research that had now revealed his significance, his power and standing being higher than that of the major king. He was friendly and told us of his call by the goddess when he was 11 years old. When John asked how he felt about being chosen by her, he manifested! – a great sepulchral throat swallowed his face in a grotesque smile. I found myself staring down this gaping throat and later recalled that's how I had described the 'spirit of sacrifice' over the island – a great yawning mouth devouring everything, swallowing it down an insatiable throat, humans and animals and living things and whatever it could devour.

"Aaagh, aaagh, I couldn't do anything about it. I just accepted it, and, yes, I'm happy."

He told us how he was 'taking dominion' (his words) over the lakes and mountains across Bali and Indonesia – and eventually the world – at the goddess' command. "This pleases the spirits and enables us to communicate with them better."

He had pilgrimaged next door to Lombok to 'take' the mountain there, and further east taking Mt Tambura, which blew up recently. He has taken each of Java's mountains going west. A group now meets with him regularly in the crater to meditate to take the world.

"What do you mean, Pak, 'take a mountain'?" I asked. He had to make living sacrifice including an ox on the summit of the mountains. (He didn't mention human sacrifice!) These are expensive exploits, but it's amazing how the goddess always provides. He explained that it was like setting up telecommunications points on the high places throughout Indonesia and the world. (Ley lines in other words! Once again we were hearing from the horse's mouth.)

He listened politely to the Gospel and was happy to let us pray God's blessing on Bali and its people. I told him that Jesus Christ the Son of the Great God above all gods was coming back to rule the earth. How good it would be if he were taking these high places in preparation for His return.

"I have no doubt he is the most powerful man in Bali, and possibly in

Indonesia and beyond," said Leslie Keegel after engaging in strong spirit combat with him all the while we were talking.

What God Did (John)

We separated into four teams next day to visit other strategic sites.

Ours was the southernmost temple, Ulu Watu. Having learned a probable occult power line linked this temple with Besakih, we stood outside and in the authority of Jesus, broke that line and asked God to reveal his Person and power to the Balinese. Some weeks later it was this temple that was struck by lightning and burned, causing over $100,000 worth of damage. A local newspaper whined, 'Why did our god allow this to happen to his temple?' Two other temples in the mountains where a team prayed were struck by falling logs. Another temple will be destroyed for development purposes, and Besakih, the mother temple, has been closed to all visitors except active worshipers since the Balinese Christians quietly repented there. At the end of the initiative everyone noticed a change of atmosphere with a significant lightening of oppression. And next morning an earthquake shook the island. Before the initiative one of those providing prayer support 'saw a dark blanket being rolled back off the island and God's light beginning to shine in'. Another saw 'a mushroom cloud of darkness lifting off the island'.

Best of all there has been spiritual renewal among some nominal Christians, including the growth of healing and deliverance meetings, and a greater responsiveness to the gospel by unbelievers. In one particularly resistant area where a team prayed, the pastor has now baptized 15 new believers! Pastors are meeting to pray, and when the government began to build a 400-foot statue to Vishnu, they were alerted to pray against it. A few weeks ago the head of the statue caught fire and burned.

All that, as I write now, was 20 years ago! The transformation in Bali is phenomenal. Instead of incense rising to other gods, all over the island worship is rising to Yahweh and His Son Yeshua. The baals have been losing their influence and Balinese are escaping from their clutches. Bali has a powerful prayer movement, and the Indonesian prayer movement now rivals that of Korea.

Leslie Keegel from Sri Lanka prophesied:
> "Bali has been given to idol worship and the worship of evil spirits .... But when the Spirit of God breaks through, the church in Bali will be the most powerfully gifted supernatural church in the world. This is God's redemptive gift and God's redemptive purpose for Bali.
> As you lift your hands to heaven, I see the rays of light emanating from your hands against the forces of darkness, and as the forces of darkness begin to clear the black clouds, I see heaven opened and the glory of God falling upon strategic territorial locations – revival and church planting and evangelism, and fruit for your ministry."

"Bless Bali"– My report written 2003.

It was my immense privilege to be sent to represent the Australian Prayer Network at "Bless Bali", the Christian response to the (first) Bali Bombing.

'Isle of the God', is what a certain Government minister accidentally proclaimed before Australian Prime Minister John Howard and the other dignitaries at the Memorial Service. Instead of 'Isle of the gods', he made a slight but very significant slip of the tongue. Yes, God is Lord of Bali.

It was an overwhelming experience to be back in Bali again as God pulled back the curtain and showed me the transformation that had been happening, and how He was fulfilling prophetic words given in 1996.

Festival of Praise

The Church of Bali has certainly caught the key to rising in victory above their circumstances. Because of the rain this celebration was moved from the Art Centre stadium to the "Valley of Praise", or Worship Centre. This is a magnificent centre just metres away from where we first started our work, 'Bali Harvest'. In fact the Lord showed me three sites where I had lived and worked which were now being used to His glory. *The places where the soles of your feet trod, I am reclaiming. They are My inheritance*, He seemed to be saying. The Bethany congregation was 2000 strong. Tears coursed down my cheeks as I listened to the gentle pre-programme worship.

Tonight choirs and music groups put on their best for Jesus. The excellence was overwhelming. One small choir was from a local music school. A slender young girl soloist was backed by a great pipe organ (taped). Her voice built till it filled the whole auditorium with the most glorious worship. I was sobbing. Once upon a time I was distressed and jealous that the gods here got all the worship. **Not any more!**

International Worship Service

Tropical rain was deluging down, but undeterred, thousands gathered in the great amphitheatre of the Art Centre. Ushered down to the very front row Julie and I huddled under a shared umbrella. The Bishop in his robes, the governor's representative and all the dignitaries sat stoically in the rain. The stage was beautifully decorated Balinese style in front of its 'temple gates' (from which a leering demon definitely took back stage!) Sound equipment was draped in plastic sheets. Mikes hung on strings in the rain. And the dancers worshipped lavishly, their magnificent dresses dragging through puddles and mud. It would never happen in Australia!

Group after group presented the highest quality performance, joyously worshipping Jesus. **Six thousand people sat under umbrellas and plastic sheets worshipping Jesus** with them, making a statement to the heavenlies: "Love Conquers Fear. We love Jesus and we bless Bali." I watched the young girls so exuberantly worshipping Jesus despite the circumstances. They are so beautiful. I couldn't help remembering that many of these young Christian women had been violated and gang raped in atrocities against the church in other parts of Indonesia - perhaps even some of these who had come. But despite the ever-present threat they were willing to gather in this significant stand against evil and abandonedly worship Jesus. Tears mingled with the rain running down my cheeks!

There were **two memorable items.** One was so impressive the Lord turned off the rain for it! Four young men marched down the aisle and up onto the stage bearing on their shoulders an enormous crown. They laid it on the stage and exuberant dancers with very skilful banners and huge streamers glorified the King of Kings. I couldn't help recalling that the last time I was at this centre was to see Queen Elizabeth. But **a greater than Queen Elizabeth is here tonight!**

The other item was a Balinese rendition of Jesus the Bridegroom. To the music of a gamelan orchestra a male Balinese dancer came slowly forward with the angular dance of the Balinese, carrying a tray of burning candles. On either side of him was a Balinese girl dressed in white, each also carrying candles. 'Jesus' laid the clusters of candles at three points across the front of the stage. There was something so majestic about it, so awesome. My mind was filled with the virgins and their lamps and the imminent return of the Groom for His Bride. The Bali Church has worked hard to contextualize the Gospel. This was most moving.

A couple of hundred bomb victims and families were present. The Governor and the Bishop made gifts to them on behalf of the Churches. After three hours the evening was called to a close because the electrical situation was getting too dangerous.

Bali Berdoa (Prayer Network)

Bali Berdoa formed after the 1996 Strategic Level Warfare. Already prayer houses operate in three provincial capitals. 200 pastors meet monthly to breakfast together. At one of these gatherings the Spirit of God convicted a major leader of his attitude towards other pastors. Repenting, he took off his belt and swapped it with that of my nephew, an apostolic leader, and they wept together. The spirit of conviction flowed across the ministers. Now a great sense of love prevails amongst them. My nephew showed me his belt which he wears always, an awesome symbol of God's grace.

Intercessors go out monthly to pray at various locations. After their visit one strategic temple was struck by lightning and severely damaged.

Some churches even have paid intercessors on staff.

A NZ friend, living here, told me that all her household has now, amidst much drama, miraculously come to the Lord. At one time an enraged man confronted her wielding a knife. "In the Name of Jesus put it down," she said. "Don't say that Name! I can't stand that Name," he screamed dropping the knife!!

Bali is no longer 'the isle of the gods'. Since Balinese leaders broke historic contracts with the powers of darkness, the atmosphere has changed. King Jesus is receiving His rightful inheritance, and His people all over the island are giving Him the worship due Him. Souls are coming to Jesus in unprecedented numbers. Ministers are praying together. Churches burst with new life. The Bomb brought unprecedented opportunity for the Gospel in Bali. Prayer has escalated again.

The word Bali comes from wali – a precious offering. Bali was a most beautiful jewel chosen from the islands of the world as a gift to the gods. But this island, once an offering to the gods, is being torn from the clutches of the evil one. It is now becoming the precious inheritance of Him Who died to redeem it. Can the prey of the terrible be released? Yes![34]

> 2005: "I gave you Bali, what are you doing about it? This is the second bomb that has brought destruction in your jurisdiction." This was a shake-up call. "You asked for Bali."

In the following chapter watch what happens when a teenager takes charge of his jurisdiction.

~

---

[34] Bless Bali Report, JA 6/12/02

Chapter 7
Take Charge
Joseph the Dreamer

Have you ever noticed how many times 'given charge' is mentioned in the story of Joseph? (Gen 41) The words 'take charge', or 'given charge' keep cropping up throughout God's history of mankind. Adam was the first one given the mandate, and it goes on from there. Let's take a look at Joseph.

Joseph's Growing Jurisdictions

Potiphar's Place

Sibling rivalry has developed into full-blown jealousy at home – and *jealousy is cruel as the grave.* (S of S 8:6)

Carrying out his father's orders, 17 year-old Joseph walks right into his brothers' murderous plot. (It's not about the coloured coat; but it is about the mantle he wears!) The brothers decide to be merciful and swap the death plot for something more lucrative.

So suddenly Joseph finds himself a slave serving in a foreign house, in a foreign country, with a foreign language, foreign culture and a pagan religion. He makes the most of a bad job and serves diligently. Potiphar is impressed.

(Joseph hasn't lost the real mantle, only the material one.) Before long the master puts him **'in charge' of everything that goes on in the house.**

Except of course Lady Potiphar!

Can you hear the God-echo: "Don't touch this tree of knowledge."? And would you believe it, Satan finds another serpent who will beguile and proffer forbidden fruit. Unlike Eve however, Joseph rejects the temptation. Where was the Human Rights Bill for this innocent young man? Without a trial, no access to a lawyer, a labour union, or even an embassy, he loses his job and is thrown into a foreign prison – from bad to worse, slave to convict.

Prison

Joseph has enjoyed eleven years of 'privilege' in Potiphar's house. Now he finds himself in jail – with Pharaoh's elite prisoners as his cell-mates.

From early childhood Joseph has been taught three things:

— how to work
— how to respect those in authority over him
— that God will never leave Him

So, as everywhere else, the Lord is with him in prison. Again he is 'a man under authority', and again God gives him favour. Wouldn't you know it, in no time the gaoler puts Joseph *'in charge' of all that goes on in the prison* – responsible for all that is done there.

Joseph assumes the responsibility of looking after the welfare of the prisoners – his companions and 'clients'.

"How are you feeling today? Why are you looking so depressed?" he asks Pharaoh's baker and wine steward.

They've both had bad dreams.

"Don't dreams belong to God?" he says. He should know! It's ultimately his dreams that got him in this mess! Joseph interprets their dreams with confidence. "By the way, when your dreams come to pass, remember me. I'm innocent here. I appeal to Pharaoh."

Palace

The baker has long been executed (as per his dream) and the butler has served many wines to Pharaoh (as per his dream) before 'Jeeves'[35] happens to remember Joseph, back there, still in charge, running the prison. This time it is Pharaoh having a bad dream. "Oh your Majesty, forgive me! I forgot Joseph, my lord. He reads dreams."

The word flies to the jail. "Get rid of his prison garb, quickly! He's to stand before Pharaoh, ruler of the world!" ("Bathe him, comb him, dress him in raiment fit for the presence of the King!" Don't you love it! Called up higher.)

"I cannot interpret, *but God will give Pharaoh an answer.*" (I love this boy!) That's a strong word (dikté) into his new jurisdiction! Joseph proceeds to both tell Pharaoh his two dreams and then interpret them. There's no stopping him now; he has a voice. In take-charge mode he goes right on to advise Pharaoh how to handle the situation, speaking wisdom into his expanded jurisdiction. After all, Pharaoh called for his help.

Pharaoh acknowledges: "One in whom is the spirit of God. There is no one so discerning and wise as you. You shall be **'in charge' of the whole land of Egypt."**

Parliament (Government)

Take a look at this for authority – yours as well as Joseph's:

> Pharaoh puts his signet ring on Joseph's finger. Whatever he speaks (dikté) from now on is to be signed with the King's ring – juris (legal) dikté. His words are as Pharaoh's words.
>
> Pharaoh dresses him in fine linen – the righteousness of the saints. The accusations and jail records are all deleted. Nothing is held against him.
>
> Pharaoh puts a gold chain round his neck – symbol of office.
>
> Pharaoh gives him the 2IC[36] chariot. Joseph is now Vice-pharaoh. Men shout before him, "Make way! Make way!"

---

35 Jeeves is a famous butler character in English literature.
36 Second In Charge

Pharaoh gives him a new name, and a wife – daughter of the high priest, the holy man.[37]

"Without your word no one will lift hand or foot in Egypt," Pharaoh declares. That sets the parameters of his jurisdiction! No one moves without his say-so in all the Empire.

The story goes on to describe how Joseph administers his jurisdiction. Taking charge of his territory, he travels back and forth throughout the land, making himself familiar with all that is going on in his domain, and making himself known to the people. He stores up huge quantities of grain, too much to keep recording. When, true to Joseph's prediction, the famine strikes the king says, "Go to Joseph and **do what he tells you.**" (God's edict is that all entities in your spiritual jurisdiction do what you tell them to. Also, when things get tough people will come to God's sons acknowledging that they will know what to do.)

So Joseph sells grain to the Egyptians.
Joseph buys everything for Pharaoh:

People buy grain first with	silver – until it is finished.
Then they use their	livestock.
Then they sell their	land.
At last they sell	themselves.

All they have and are becomes Pharaoh's property, and they are given grain to eat and to plant. (Is this not our jurisdictional aim, that all become God's precious possession and are provided for by Him?) Of everything the people subsequently produce, one-fifth is to be returned to Pharaoh, because in fact he owns it all.

So Joseph bought all the land in Egypt for Pharaoh. (Gen 47:20)
Only the land of the priests does not become Pharaoh's,

---

37 It's outside the scope of this book to look into these beautiful symbols, but I can't help highlighting some of them as an enticement for you to look again at what the Father endows on His sons and heirs.

because Pharaoh supplies them from his own table and they don't need to sell all they own to buy food to survive. (We too are supplied from the King's table and will not be reduced to servitude in hard times.)

Besides all this, '*All the countries came to buy grain from Joseph*' because the famine he prophesied has indeed touched all the world. This son's jurisdiction is becoming global!

Patriarchy (The family)

Joseph's old father, Jacob, knowing nothing of his son's fortunes, sends Judah ahead of the family to the great Vice-Pharaoh, Zaphenath-Paneah (Joseph), to get advice.[38]

The result is family reconciliation, healing and provision. Joseph's vision has never been restricted to current circumstances; he sees the eternal, Kingdom picture – God meant it for good. "Never mind about your things, because the best of all Egypt will be yours." Joseph gives them property in the choicest part of the land. I find it interesting that Benjamin's portion was five times as much as anyone else's. (There's a blessing of great grace on this last generation – the youth.[39])

What Does All This Mean to You?

Joseph is a stranger in a strange land, raised by God's presence in him to be governor of that land. We too are living in Egypt, the physical world around us, but are citizens of another kingdom whose ruler is God. Here in this foreign realm God gives us growing authority as we represent Him. It is His intention that the whole of Egypt be bought for Him – that nothing happens without our word as we act on His behalf, mantled in His robe of authority and wearing His ring with which to seal the edicts we make on His behalf. We have been given responsibility for everything that is done in this realm. It is our role to bring Heaven's dominion to earth.

---

38 Gen 46
39 See chapter 3

God says: *Concerning the works of My hands, you command Me.* (Isa 45:11 NKJV) And, *You will also declare a thing and it will be established for you.* (Job 22:28 NKJV)

It's a great shame that many of God's children have whined away in the wilderness instead of arising to **take charge** of their circumstances and bring about God's order and blessing where they are. In the household or community where God has planted you He wants you to be in charge, bringing about His will, His blessing and His order.

And His promise is that in times of trouble what affects Egypt will not harm you; He is your provider and sustainer. What a gracious God! He deserves all the worship. He deserves the Nations for His inheritance.

Prayer

Forgive us Lord, we have been drivelling beggars instead of the rulers You called us to be. Help us King Jesus to be worthy regents, representing your Kingdom reign and establishing Your Lordship. Help us to comprehend the responsibility You have committed to us and act upon Your plans for us to subdue the earth and the kingdoms of darkness in Your Name.

Your jurisdiction is the area of influence God has given you over which to establish His dominion. Take charge of it.

~

Chapter 8
Take Charge
Esther the Orphan

Esther was another teenager who stepped up and took charge of an extraordinary jurisdiction. I'm sure she had no ambitions to be Queen of the known world or to change the course of history. How often we tumble almost by accident into roles we never dreamed of.

History - Building the Jurisdiction

Let me fill you in on a little of the tumultuous background and the royal blood lines converging in this young girl's destiny. (If history's not your thing feel free to skip to 'Mordecai and Esther' after the map. However, bear in mind the next few pages will describe the evolution of the vast jurisdiction God was preparing for this orphan girl to inherit.)

From historical accounts I calculate that Esther must be about twelve years old when we meet her and she is taken into King Xerxes' harem in Iran.[40]

---

[40] Some historians place Esther with Artaxerxes — an unlikely generation later. When historians differ, my next preferred extra-Biblical source is Josephus' historical record. Josephus was a respected Jewish historian contemporary with the Apostles (c. AD 37–100).

King Nebuchadnezzar (ruled 597–562 BC[41])

Esther is a *bene gola,* meaning a descendant of the 'Stolen Generation' captured from Jerusalem by King Nebuchadnezzar more than a century ago. Nebuchadnezzar took hostage the best minds and artisans of Judah, its nobles and officials, along with their king, Jehoiachin. Esther's great-grandparents and a young Ezekiel were among 10,000 prisoners of war he herded to Babylon, Iran, capital of the Chaldean Empire.

Esther has listened over and over to the stories passed down from her grandparents and her parents, and now regularly retold by Mordecai. They are part of the fabric of her being – who she is. Among the many stories of Exile her favourite is of Daniel, one of the Stolen Generation (*bene gola*) who became 2IC of the Babylonian Empire. Rivals had him thrown to the lions under King Darius, but the God of their fathers Abraham, Isaac and Jacob saved him. The most memorable story is of that tortuous trek her great-grandparents made, shuffling shackled for months across deserts and mountains to Babylon. En route they served as best they could their beloved King Jehoiachin, son of King Josiah.

They were the lucky ones. Scarcely a decade later Nebuchadnezzar, provoked by their rebellion, starved and totally destroyed everyone and everything in Jerusalem, including their Holy Temple. King Zedekiah was blinded and hurled into a Babylonian prison joining his nephew, Jehoiachin. The remnant *bene gola* in exile and their offspring became stateless – Judah, their homeland, no longer existed.

But the Prophet Jeremiah wrote to God's scattered people encouraging them to make themselves at home in Iran (Chaldea), because captivity would last a life-time (70 years). So the exiles accepted positions in Nebuchadnezzar's administration and assimilated as best they could into Babylonian society. Esther's grandparents were likely some of these displaced Jews who formed a community to remember their spiritual traditions and follow God's instructions to them as His chosen people.

---

41 Dates are approximate estimates by historians and not always verifiable.

They witnessed the destabilizing seven years of Nebuchadnezzar's insanity and his miraculous healing, and no doubt thrilled at his subsequent declarations of '*the supremacy and power of the God of Heaven*'. Unfortunately Nebuchadnezzar died shortly after this, succeeded briefly by his son Evil Merodach (who released and befriended his father's political prisoner, King Jehoiachin). Coups, murders and successors traipsed through the royal city over the next few years, until Cyrus the Great of Persia conquered the Chaldean (Babylonian) Empire without a battle. (While King Belshazzar partied, Cyrus' engineers diverted the Euphrates River which the city straddled, drained its protective moats and entered unchallenged! An ingenious feat of engineering.)

Cyrus the Great (ruled 559–530 BC)

150 years before Cyrus' birth the Jewish prophet, Isaiah, had named the Persian King Cyrus, and predicted his destiny as God's chosen ruler and deliverer of His Jewish people. When King Cyrus married Queen Cassandane of Media (550 BC) the great Median and Persian Empires united.

Cyrus officially ended the Jewish Exile (c. 538 BC) and decreed that all Jews were free to return to Jerusalem. He ordered them to rebuild the Temple and re-establish worship there to the God of Heaven. Many however preferred to stay in their current comfort. For the few who caught the vision and obeyed, it was long hard labour, continuing into (and beyond) the time of Mordecai.

Cyrus believed the final epic battle between Good and Evil was approaching and that Persia would bring about the triumph of Good. For this reason he wanted to conquer all peoples and set the stage for the final triumph of Good.[42] As a result Cyrus's Empire was larger than any that had yet existed and he was the greatest conqueror yet known.

This is important to note, because this was the jurisdiction God set up for another most unlikely chosen instrument, a little *bene gola,* Esther.

---

42   www.jewishvirtuallibrary.org/jsource/History/Exile1.html/After the Babylonian Empire. Note: Josephus makes no mention of Cyrus' Zoroastrian beliefs but honours him as a believer in Yahweh Who communicates with him.

Cambyses II (ruled 530–522 BC)

Cyrus' son, Cambyses, added Egypt to his father's Empire, carrying the Pharaoh off to Susa, his new capital. Cambyses halted the rebuilding of Jerusalem, on complaints from neighbouring states. He was however killed in battle and a bizarre turn of events followed. A look-alike imposter took the throne (and his wives!) for a period. Cambyses' uncle (brother of the Queen[43]) came to the rescue and, with Darius, exposed and overthrew the pretender.

Darius the Great (ruled 522–486 BC)

Darius was a relative of Cyrus and a general in Cambyses' army. In the power vacuum, Cambyses' uncle established Darius as Cyrus' successor.

It happened that two of the royal women abused by the imposter were first cousins, one a niece and one a daughter of Cyrus – one Cambyses' Queen, Phaidymia, and the other Cambyses' sister, Atossa. Darius took both of these women in and married them. It is entirely possible that these two powerful royals are still residing (if not presiding) in the Palace when Esther enters.

Darius reasserted Cyrus' decrees about rebuilding Jerusalem and the Temple, and assisted over 42,000 more Jews to return to their homeland. Zerubbabel, Governor of Jerusalem, was his personal friend and Daniel, now a very old man, his close advisor. Darius too made Empirical edicts:

> *To all peoples, nations, and languages that dwell in all the earth: I make a decree that in every dominion of my kingdom men must tremble and fear before the God of Daniel. For He is the living God, and steadfast forever; His kingdom is the one which shall not be destroyed, and His dominion shall endure to the end.* (Dan 6:25, 26 NKJV)

There is a reason why Darius was called 'Darius the Great'. He expanded and stabilized the Empire, allowing conquered peoples to continue their traditions. He centralized administration, made legal reforms and organized judicial systems. He created provinces with satraps

---

43 Queen Cassandane

and built roads to every province. He designed a uniform money system, encouraged arts, and made Aramaic the official language of the Empire.

When Darius' health began to fail he chose Xerxes, son of his wife Atossa,[44] as his successor.

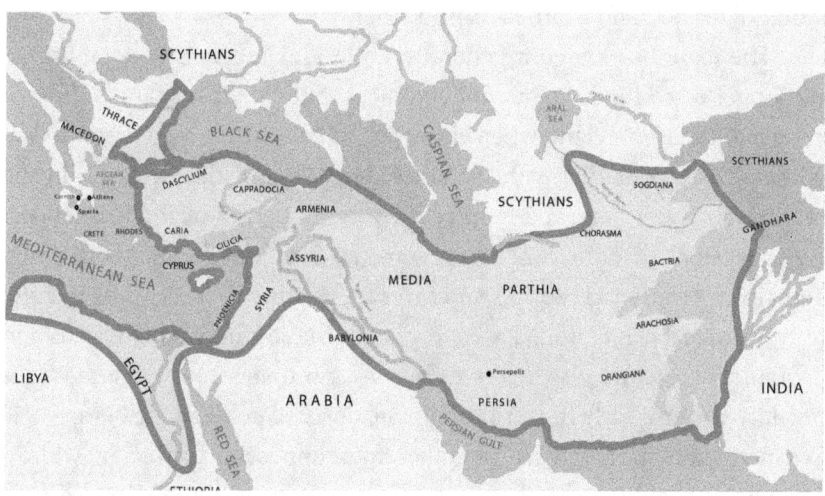

Xerxes the Great (ruled 486–465 BC)

Enter Xerxes (King Ahasuerus), son of Darius the Great, grandson of Cyrus the Great, ruler of the great Medo-Persian Empire with his capital in Susa,[45] 200 miles east of Babylon. Xerxes is around 35 at the time of his accession. His Empire reaches from India to Ethiopia, 127 'Provinces'. His military power is 2,000,000 strong supplemented by a navy of 4000 ships.

Mordecai and Esther

Mordecai and Esther's genealogies are not nearly as illustrious. They can claim a dubious relationship to King Saul of Israel, being descendants of Saul's nephew, Shimei. Shimei was infamous for his vendetta against King David and cursed him bitterly in a vulnerable time. Although David graciously

---

44 Daughter of Cyrus the Great
45 Sometimes called Shushan, now known as Shush in Iran.

spared his life, later King Solomon had to deal with his insurrection.

It is interesting to note that had David not forgiven Shimei at the time, there would have been no Mordecai and Esther.

> Had David not forgiven Shimei there may have been no Mordecai or Esther.

The exile has ended a generation ago and Judah is re-established, no longer as a kingdom, but a theological state.[46] Esther's family did not return to their homeland when either Cyrus or Darius urged them to. The Midrash[47] suggests that Esther's father died while Esther was still in the womb. Then her bereaved mother died in giving her birth. This left the newborn Esther to the care of her cousin, Mordecai, seemingly her only remaining relative. He adopts and cares for the tiny baby as his own child.

Mordecai is mentioned as a prophet in the second year of Darius and rabbinical literature also refers to him as a prophet.[48] We presume he is wealthy because early in Darius' reign he donated gold for the Temple. He is a member of the Sanhedrin, and therefore supposedly conversant with 70 languages. That he sits in the King's gate means he is in the King's service. He would be privy to the personalities and intrigues of the royal court and most likely attends the great party thrown in the third year of Xerxes' reign.

The Feast

Three years into his reign Xerxes throws a royal banquet. It is an extraordinary feast. It lasts 180 days. I don't suppose everyone sat and gorged for 180 days. I imagine Xerxes' administrative skills would have streams of his princes and nobles from India to Spain, along with Median and Persian military officers and governors, rostering in from the provinces throughout the six months. There are 127 provinces remember. He is making sure they see the *riches of his glorious kingdom, the splendour*

---

46 Jewish Virtual Library/After the Babylonian Exile <https://www.jewishvirtuallibrary.org/jsource/History/Exile1.html> accessed 27 June 2015
47 (Esth. Rabbah 6:5; BT Megillah 13a)
<http://jwa.org/encyclopedia/article/esther-midrash-and-aggadah>
48 (Meg. 10b, 15a; Ḥul. 139b)

and excellence of his majesty.[49] (Sound prophetic to you?)

Then the King extends his generosity a further seven days for the people in his home town, Susa. Everyone, least to greatest, is invited. The feast is held in the garden of the king's palace. (Some have even suggested that this was in fact the site of the famous Hanging Gardens.) The opulence! Just for the everyday mums and dads! The guests may enjoy the largesse of the King at their pleasure.

On the seventh and climax day of the Feast the King is seriously missing his Queen. *When the King's heart was happy with wine* ... He wants to show the princes and the peoples how exquisite his Bride is. He calls for her. It's been a long 187 days. "It's time to come, Darling!"

Queen Vashti is actually Xerxes' first cousin and she is throwing a party for the women, busy hosting her own celebrations. The dowager Queens may even be there with all their pomp. Vashti refuses to come to her husband's drunken party. I must confess I have always felt she was quite justified. I've felt indignant for her, being called to front up to a debauched mob for their lecherous entertainment. But as I write I am seeing something quite different. Xerxes actually called himself 'King of kings'. I see the King of an unseen Kingdom throwing a lavish party for all His subjects, then longing for His Bride. He wants His glorious Bride at His side. He wants to show her off proudly to everyone. But she refuses to come – and

> The ornate extravaganza! Just for the ordinary mums and dads. Festoons of multiple, coloured hangings fastened with silver rings, marble pillars, couches of gold and silver on porphyry pavement, white marble walls set with mother-of-pearl and precious coloured stones. Royal wine flowing liberally, savoured from golden goblets of unique design – and no drinking restrictions, or obligations.

---

49   Esth 1:4 NKJV

ultimately her place is given to another. It's sobering.[50]

Xerxes is persuaded by his courtiers to divorce Vashti. Let not the Queen's example encourage insurrection among other wives! It could be a great disaster for the Empire (not to mention them)! Make an example of her, they urge.

At least Vashti is only banished and not beheaded as is happening in the same region today!

But Xerxes truly misses his wife, falling into such depression that his counsellors have to figure a way to lift him out of it. This is the catalyst for the search – present every beautiful virgin from across the Empire before the King.

Twelve-year-old Esther is stunningly beautiful. Her personal tragedies have produced in her a rare maturity. Now, in the protection of her devoted and devout cousin's home she is quietly secure in her own identity as one of God's chosen people.

Mordecai knows there is no hiding her. He does his best to prepare her for the culture shock to come, and warns her not to disclose her Jewish heritage. The inevitable knock comes on the door for Cinderella. There is no denying the will of the Emperor.

Jurisdictional Changes

The first expansion of Esther's jurisdiction is the leap from the shelter of Mordecai's home to Xerxes' harem.

The Harem

If she is terrified, Esther doesn't show it. That she is confident God controls her destiny, gives her a composure that sets her apart from the mêlée of beauties clamouring to be queen. Esther stands out from the 400 entrants in this beauty pageant. The loveliness of her character charms everyone,

---

50 A 'type', is something real in earth terms which pictures something in another reality or time. This incident may not be an intentional type, but it reminds me of the End of Time when the Heavenly Bridegroom calls His spiritual Bride to the 'marriage supper of the Lamb'. (Rev 19:7.) Not all respond.

and her unaffected grace immediately wins the favour of the official in charge of the harem. He processes her at once, appoints her seven of the King's servant girls and escorts her out of the check-in clamour, settling her in the best apartment in the harem.

This is beyond the wildest teenage dream. The extravagant indulgence! Hegai, manager of the harem, loads her girls with all the best diet foods and the most exquisite cosmetics – the latest, most highly recommended potions and enhancements from the world's top merchants. Teeth to toenails to tummy are meticulously tended. Her girls are wonderful masseurs. For six months they ritually cleanse and bathe and scrub her with exotic spices and husks. A further six months they pamper her in baths of perfumed oils – and more luxurious massages.

After a year her time of preparation is over; she is called before the King. Unlike other contestants demanding the earth, Esther asks for nothing more than Hegai deems appropriate for her to bring to the King's chamber. And favour accompanies her again. She needs nothing in addition to the favour of the Lord. The King is stunned with her dignity, her natural elegance and her unselfconscious beauty. It is recorded, *he fell in love with the damsel.*[51]

The Palace

After this epochal night of intimacy with the King, Esther never again returns to the virgins' harem under Hegai. Her life has changed forever. She now resides in the concubines' quarters – until such time as the King can make arrangements for their wedding. Xerxes throws another feast, and this time it's for Esther. He proclaims a holiday for all the people in his domain and distributes presents. Esther is escorted with great grandeur to the Palace where the Emperor legally marries her, places a crown on her head and pronounces her **Queen of the Empire.**

---

51   The Works of Josephus, p298, 1987 Hendrickson Publishers.

The Throne

Esther knows she is riding on an awesome current of divine destiny. It holds her steady through all the mind-swirling adjustments – to people, place, position, and power.

She moves into the apartments in the Palace, elaborately redecorated just for her. Her relationship with the King builds and they share matters of heart and state.

All this time Mordecai has kept a daily vigil at the Gate of the palace to make sure that his beloved cousin is not suffering abuse in this foreign court. Communication lines run through Esther's trusted servants. One day Mordecai is awaiting her news when he overhears two servants angrily plotting against the King. (His knowledge of languages, specifically the language of Tarshish from which the two derive, enables Mordecai to understand the plot.[52]) He immediately informs Esther, who warns the King, and the plot is averted. The King himself, being her husband, has now come within Esther's jurisdiction, and she saves his life – and ultimately the fate of the Empire.

Mordecai, in the King's gate, is a fine intelligence agent, keeping his cousin informed of events across the Empire.

Soon there is another plot. Xerxes' favourite courtier, Haman, whom he has elevated to vice-Emperor, is infuriated with Mordecai. This Jew refuses to kow-tow to him as everyone else does. He persuades the King that there is an ethnic group in his realm which is insurrectionist and dangerous to the King's rule and he should get rid of them; he, Haman, will pay all expenses. So Haman gains permission and sends an edict across the Empire, stamped with the Emperor's seal. 'Death Penalty to all Jews. On the day of 13/12/12 all Jews are to be executed, man, woman and child.'

The King and Haman sat down to drink but the city Shushan was in

---

52 (Meg. 13b; comp. Targum Sheni to Esth. ii. 22). <http://www.jewishencyclopedia.com/articles/10983-mordecai>

turmoil.[53] I have always been struck by the power of this statement. How often leaders in their ivory towers make decisions quite oblivious of the effect they will have on their people, the human tragedies they have inflicted.

Mordecai and his fellow-Jews immediately revert to their ethnic expressions of grief. They dress themselves in sugarbags, pour ashes over their heads and beards and wail inconsolably in the public square. Esther sends her maids to dress her cousin properly, but he ignores them. When she finally sends Hathach, the Personal Assistant appointed to her by the King, Mordecai responds. This is a serious matter – national security stuff. It can only be entrusted to proven officials with direct access to the High Court.

Mordecai sends a copy of the edict to his cousin along with this message:

"This is your jurisdiction. It is happening on your watch and you must act to stop it."

Esther responds, "I can't, I haven't been invited. Not for a month now. I could get my head cut off." (It is true that guarding the Throne are security men with mean axes to make sure no one uninvited enters the Throne Room, or approaches the Emperor.)

Mordecai answers in no uncertain terms. "We are all about to be massacred, you included. Why do you think God has put you in this position? There is a purpose to where He puts you. If you don't take charge now and deliver your people, God will find someone else, but you won't be around to see it."

The Jews

Esther has always respected and obeyed Mordecai. She knows she is not here by chance. God's destiny cloaks her like a mantle. She has always felt it. "My staff and I will fast. Call all the people to fast and pray three days for me. I will go to the King. And if I die for it, I die."

All the Jews in Susa, and as many outside as hear the call, obey her. This is her first dikté to her own people.

---

53 Esth 3:15

The Court of the King

Her palace attendants nervously help her dress in her royal ceremonial robes and her crown. With a maid at her side to support her and a second carrying the heavy train she approaches the Throne Room. There she waits with regal decorum outside the entrance, honouring the King with true deference (and not a little terror). It has always been her inner loveliness which has won her favour with everyone.

The King cannot resist her, especially when, according to Josephus, she swoons with fear on approaching his 'terrible majesty'. Although her maid steadies her, the King leaps from his Throne and takes her in his arms assuring her that the 'law of no approach' is for his subjects, but she is Queen as he is King; she is entirely safe. He presses the sceptre into her hands and lays his ceremonial rod of acceptance on her neck to free her from fear.

I find this report of Josephus' so delightful I share it with you.

> *After she had recovered herself by these encouragements, she said, "My Lord, it is not easy for me on the sudden, to say what hath happened, for so soon as I saw thee to be great, and comely, and terrible, my spirit departed from me, and I had no soul left in me."*
>
> *And while it was with difficulty and in a low voice that she could say this much, the king was in great agony and disorder, and encouraged Esther to be of good cheer, and to expect better fortune, since he was ready, if occasion should require it, to grant her the half of his kingdom.*[54]

So on recovering sufficiently she requests that the King with his chief courtier, Haman, come to a supper she has prepared for them. He promptly agrees, then at the banquet asks her what is on her mind; he will not disappoint her even if she asks for half his Empire. It's been a big day. Esther defers. Would he and Haman mind coming again next day and she will speak her heart?

---

54 The Works of Josephus. (c. AD 37–100) Transl. Whiston, 1763. Pub. Hendrickson © 1987. Bk 2, Ch 6: 240, 241.

During the night two invisible kingdoms are busy preparing for the show-down – the enemy's persistent plan to wipe out God's chosen people and destroy the line of a Redeemer has once again been activated.

Haman, gloating in his 'favour' with the Queen and drinking with his mates, supervises the building of gallows on which to hang Mordecai.

On the other hand Xerxes in the Palace can't sleep. "Bring me the chronicles." His secretaries spend the night reading him the historical records of the Empire.

"Mordecai saved my life. How was he rewarded for that?"

"No, your Majesty, no reward was paid him."

So it happened that Haman, arriving bright-eyed in the morning, is unceremoniously designated the task of honouring his enemy, Mordecai. Mortified after his city tour, leading Mordecai mounted in state on the King's steed, Haman hurries to the second banquet with the Queen.

"So my Queen, what is on your heart?" asks the King again. "You shall have whatever you request, to the half of my dominion."

Esther pours out passionately the dilemma of her people, revealing for the first time her Jewish heritage.

"What monster would contrive a genocide like this in my jurisdiction?" rages the King.

"None other than the King's trusted prime minister, this Haman, your Majesty."

The King stands abruptly from the table and strides out to deal with his shock and rage. Haman falls grovelling on the Queen's couch begging for mercy.

"Will he even molest the Queen before my very eyes!" shouts the King, returning.

The servants pull a sack over Haman's head and lead him out. "See the gallows Haman made for Mordecai, Majesty," they point out.

"Hang him on them!"

The Empire

But this is not the end of the matter. Esther has to persist and approach the King again to sort the practical issues. These now extend to the ends of his Empire. The King's seal has validated the order to massacre every Jew in his domain. The edict cannot be revoked.

The King honours her, appreciating her wisdom and acuity. He gives her his seal. She can write (words) whatever she wishes and sign it with his signature. So Esther and Mordecai write an *e-dikt* to counter the first and to turn the tables on their enemies. Translated into every language of the realm, letters are sent on the fastest horses to every corner of the Empire. Every Jew has permission to defend himself, his family and his property and to destroy his enemies.

Now Esther's dikté goes beyond her Jewish jurisdiction. Every governor and every official in every province relays the message to his constituency. Everyone hears – and fears. The fear of God follows the decrees of the Queen. (Our words with the King's seal evoke fear on the part of the enemy, and the fear of God fills our sphere of influence.)

The result is, anti-Semitism is wiped out of the Empire – all Jew-haters are destroyed.

The King brings the results to Esther. "Are you satisfied, my beloved Queen? Is there anything else?"

Esther knows there is much hidden jealousy and animosity in the city. "Give them an extra day in the city," she requests, "to deal with any remaining hatred. And let Haman's sons too be hanged for an example of what happens to those who oppose God's people." The King grants her request. She is reigning alongside him, making imperial edicts that bring the King's dominion over every aspect of his realm.

Esther's words defeated the plot to destroy the blood-line of the coming Redeemer, yet some 400 years away. Rising to her responsibility in this unprecedented jurisdiction Esther changes the course of history forever.

No wonder the feast of Purim is celebrated across the globe to this day, remembering when one young girl with God turned the destiny of mankind.

Although God is not directly mentioned in her story, I believe the Book of Esther provides us an example of the authority we are given not only to access the King and enjoy an intimate relationship with Him, but to rule alongside God in His Kingdom.

> *Thus says the Lord of hosts: If you will walk in my ways and keep my charge, then also you shall rule my house and have charge of my courts, and I will give you access to My Presence and places to walk among these who stand here.* (Zech 3:7. Amp.)

In the next chapter we will look at the dikté component of this authority – the power of words.

~

Chapter 9
Your Diction In Your Jurisdiction
'Speak the Word Only'

Dr Len Jones was a true Apostle before it was fashionable to be so named. An Australian/New Zealander, he first founded the Slavic and Oriental Mission supporting missionaries in Europe and Japan. His jurisdiction grew until the Mission he founded is now known as World Outreach, supporting missionaries all over the world.

In my first term on the mission field it was one of the highlights of our year to have a visit from the Director. Of the many sermons I have sat through in my life I remember very few. But Dr Jones' messages were all eminently memorable. To this day I remember the titles – 'Don't Park Here'; 'You Can'; 'Christ in You'; 'You in Christ'; 'Grace is not a Flimsy Thing'. But none was as impacting as 'Speak the Word Only'.

Would you indulge me to divert a tiny bit off the Jurisdiction track to drop by a delightful story about his message 'You Can'? (If not, feel free to drop down to the next paragraph.)

Dr Jones was growing enthusiastic about 'You can'. The village people loved him. They were sitting on mats listening with rapt attention as a Christian hotel manager interpreted his English message into Indonesian. The villagers then performed the mental acrobatics to their own language. The anointing of God was heavy and everyone was getting excited, especially the interpreter. He would beam at Dr Jones and respond with an enthusiastic "Puji Tuhan!". So the speaker would repeat his sentence. "Praise the Lord!" enthused the interpreter again. On the third repeat he'd realize, "Oops!" and drop back into his interpreter role to pass the next words on to the people. This happened so frequently that Dr Jones eventually bypassed the interpreter altogether and spoke directly to the eager village folk. I don't know what language they were hearing in, but they hung on and responded to his every word. "Say, 'I can,'" the preacher told them. "Ai gan," they repeated enthusiastically, "Ai gan!" over and over. A riot of joy flooded the venue as they received directly from the Lord. God doesn't need an interpreter! Ezra 6:22 says, God had plunged them into a sea of joy. (Well, the story was about proclaiming His words, so we didn't digress after all!)

My favourite message was when Dr Jones told the story of the centurion.[55] "You don't need to spend your time and energy to come to my place," said the Captain. "Just speak the word only and my servant will be healed." And sure enough the servant was healed at that moment back at the house.

This military leader understood two things: authority, and the power of the word.

Under Authority

He knew that his own authority, and the reason his men obeyed him, was because of the authority over him to which he submitted. If you have submitted yourself to the authority of the King of Kings you are in His chain

---

55 Mat 8; Lk 7:7

of command in His spiritual Kingdom. Whatever He has placed under your feet, or in your jurisdiction, must obey you. We are Regents of the King, acting on His behalf. *Our standing in the world is identical with Christ's.* (1Jn 4:17)

It's like having a Power of Attorney. Remember my series of three spiritual warfare dreams (chapter 4)? I held a cardboard cylinder in my hand when I opposed the attackers. I came to understand that the cylinder represented my Power of Attorney, the proof of my right to act on behalf of the One who granted me the right.

When Jesus' seventy sent-ones came back excited, saying, *"Master, even the demons danced to your tune!"* Jesus said, *"I know. I saw Satan fall, a bolt of lightning out of the sky. See what I've given you? ... All the same, the great triumph is not your authority over evil, but in God's authority over you and presence with you."* (Lk 10:17-20)

Joseph bought everything in the name of Pharaoh and for the King. In Joseph's jurisdiction everything – land, produce, animals, people – became the possession of the King.

Esther and Mordecai were given the King's seal, proof that the words so sealed were from the King. They carefully crafted decrees which did not cross or override the King's words. Their edicts were carefully aligned to the King's wishes for His dominion. They operated and decreed under His authority. The Centurion and Jesus both understood this concept.

Power of the Word

The officer also understood that in Jesus' spiritual kingdom the Word was omnipotent – all powerful. He may not have known that it was the explosive force which had set creation rolling. It was not only eternal, unstoppable, irrevocable, but it was incontestable and invincible.

I wonder if he knew he was actually talking to the Word Himself. "Speak the word only," he said to the Word Himself! What a catalyst that was. Of course his servant was healed. He couldn't not be. He had a word from the Word Himself!

Nothing and no one is impervious to God's Word. We can't get away from it – no matter what. (Heb 4: 13)

Every miracle Jesus performed was through a word. "Fill the jars!" "Wash in the pool!" "Stretch out your arm!" "Lazarus, come out!" "I say to you, 'Arise!'" Notice they're all commands. Commands are words.

We know God spoke and it was. By the Word of the Lord the heavens were made. He spoke and it was done; He commanded and it stood fast. (Ps 33:6, 9 NKJV)

But look at this: Jesus said to His followers, *"...Let him **say** (for instance to this mountain) ... whoever shall **say** ... he will have whatever he **says**."* (Mk 11:23 NKJV) Note, He didn't say 'pray'.

Dr Jones said, *For every one place you can show me in the Scriptures where things happened through PRAYING, I will show you many more where things happened through SAYING.*[56]

That's not to lessen the focus on prayer, but to encourage you to take charge and speak with the authority you have been given.

The Word Creates Cash

Following this visit of Dr Jones I was bemoaning to the Lord the fact that I didn't even have enough money to buy stamps for a letter home. (My board and lodging was covered by my teaching the children of the missionaries with whom I served. Other needs were 'by faith'.) I'd been penniless for a while. I was out of contact with home and to restore communication I needed money. It was this that prompted action.

I looked in my satchel, and checked through my drawers to make sure there weren't any odd notes hidden away and forgotten. Nothing.

That 'Speak the word only' message from the Apostle of Faith had impacted me strongly. Now was the time to practise it. "Lord," I prayed, "I am the King's daughter and You own the cattle on a thousand hills. It isn't right that Your daughter be in this situation. It is embarrassing to both me and You." Then I commanded, "Let there be money for me in the morning."

My 12-year-old roommate came in for bed. "Look at this, Glen," I

---

56 'Confess It', Len J Jones, Slavic and Oriental Mission, 1964 (Emphasis his.)

moaned, showing her into my empty satchel. "I am totally broke." Our two pairs of commiserating eyes gazed in. She didn't have any money either. That was the third time a pair of eyes had scoured the satchel.

We slept an undisturbed night. Next morning I woke excited.

"Oh yes, Lord, the money!"

Swinging my feet out of bed, I hurried over to my satchel, put in my hand and pulled out a wad of notes – Indonesian rupiahs from God's Own heavenly mint and delivered by His Own heavenly messenger during the night. Glen and I had both peered into that bare leather pocket last night. God has a mint of every currency in the world.

I really don't know why I didn't expect the money to come through the mail or in some conventional way. That's just the way it happened. God's Word is powerful and creative.

> God's Word in our mouths has limitless untapped creative power.

Some nine months later I was again rupiahless. "Let there be money for me in the morning," I dikté-ed again.

In the morning, as before, I climbed eagerly out of bed. "Yes Lord, the money. Now I wonder where You put it." I went to my regular purse. That was empty. The Lord knows where I keep my money so that's where I expected Him to put it. I looked in my other purse, but that too was empty. I had a third purse which was only ever used if the exchange of my dollars produced too fat a wad of valueless rupiahs. I looked in there, but that too was empty.

I stood in the middle of the room nonplussed. "But God CAN'T fail. He CAN'T fail. Well, maybe He's testing my faith. Maybe He's put it there since I looked." Once again I opened my regular purse. It was empty.

"But Lord, You CAN'T fail!" It is impossible for God to fail. He is GOD.

As I stood there perplexed in the middle of the room, my eyes fell on my satchel. It had been some time since I'd last used it. I knew immediately it was there. I put in my hand and pulled out a wad of rupiahs. God's word in our mouths has limitless untapped creative power.

"Are You Sure?"

"How can I be sure it's His word?" you ask.

Well first up, He lives in you doesn't He? You are a body for Him to live through. You don't live for yourself or with agendas for you. Like the centurion, you're under His authority, and He has given you authority to rule in the jurisdiction He's allocated to you.

Who can speak and have it happen if the Lord has not decreed it? (Lam 3:37 NIV) God said to Jeremiah who had similar questions, *If you speak good words rather than worthless ones, you will be my spokesman. You must influence them; do not let them influence you.* (Jer 15:19 NLT)

David's last words are recorded in 2 Samuel 23:1-7. He describes how he ruled his God-given jurisdiction. In that description (read it, it will inspire you.) are these words: **God's spirit** *spoke through me, his words took shape on my tongue.*

When Peter said, "Rise up and walk!" the people asked, "By what power are you doing this? In whose name do you dikté?" They asked Jesus the same question, and the apostles the same – "Who are you; by what authority do you speak and act?" Your authority is identical with theirs.

David Wilkerson has this to say:

> *The apostle Peter was made of flesh and blood, just like the rest of us. Yet he wielded spiritual authority over the devil. He said to the lame man at the temple gate, "In the name of Jesus Christ of Nazareth rise up and walk!" (Acts 3:6),[57] and the man was healed. The religious leaders of the day recognized this power in Peter and asked him, "By what power, or by what name, have ye done this?" (Acts 4:7)*
>
> *Nowhere does the Bible suggest that this same power isn't meant for us today. When did the Lord ever say to His Church, "I've helped you so far. Now you're on your own"? What kind of God would empower His people in the wilderness when they needed it – would empower*

---

57 Wilkerson quotes from KJV.

Israel's kings, prophets like Elijah, the crowds at Pentecost – and then withhold it from His last-days Church, when we need it more than any generation?

According to Scripture, Satan's power has increased in our day: "The devil is come down unto you, having great wrath, because he knoweth that he hath but a short time." (Rev 12:12) Why would God permit Satan to attack a weak, powerless church that has no defence? His people have never lost access to His divine power.[58]

Use the S-word

Don't let the enemy intimidate you or steal your confidence to speak. You know that God has given us armour which is **battle** gear, so don't be surprised to find yourself in a war. The armour is defensive gear for protection. (God-of-the-Angel-Armies **expects** you to be shot at!) He has given us only one weapon of offence – the sword, which is the WORD. He makes it clear the sword is the sword **of the Spirit.** This is not a physical war; it's a **spirit**ual war. So our one weapon is the Spirit Word. *Life and death are in the power of the tongue,* Solomon says.
Words:

— Kill or Give Life,
— Murder or Revive
— Create or Destroy
— Build or Tear down

And God has entrusted us with this authority – this incontestable, invincible weapon! This is more powerful than any of the awesome weapons we see in movies. Those are just a poor attempt to imitate God's limitless, irresistible power. What manner of persons ought we to be? You have a GOD-sword – God's-word!

Jeremiah says, *A curse on him who is lax in doing the Lord's work! A*

---

58 <http://sermons.worldchallenge.org/en/node/32700>

curse on him who keeps his sword from bloodshed!' (Jer 48:10 NIV) (But also *a curse on him who assassinates people with the tongue*.[59] Our war is not against flesh and blood, but against spiritual powers.[60]) *Say only what helps, each word a gift.* (Eph 4:29)

What can you speak to?

What do you have authority over? Where do your words take effect? What 'juris' can you 'dikté' over?

Five kingdoms are amassed to attack the city of Gibeon (Josh 10) so the frightened Gibeonites call Joshua. Joshua sets out and marches his whole army all night and God says, *"Don't give them a second thought. I've put them under your thumb – not one of them will stand up to you."* (v. 8)

Joshua is encouraged, takes the five armies by surprise and engages them in a brutal battle. But the battle seems endless, relentless numbers more keep replacing the vanquished. The sun is about to set and Joshua needs more time to complete the victory.

> *So, Joshua spoke to God with all Israel listening:*
> *"Stop, Sun, over Gibeon. Halt, Moon, over Aijalon Valley."*
> *And Sun stopped, Moon stood still, until he defeated his enemies.*
> *The sun stopped in its tracks in mid sky; just sat there all day.*
> *There's never been a day like that before or since – God took orders from a human voice! Truly, God fought for Israel.* (vv. 12, 13)

Joshua keeps speaking into the situation. The five kings have escaped and holed up in a cave. *"Roll big stones against the mouth of the cave and post guards to keep watch. But don't you hang around – go after your enemies. Cut off their retreat. Don't let them back into their cities. God has given them to you."* (vv. 18, 19)

Joshua had amazing faith. God had said not one of his enemies

---

59 Jas 3
60 Eph 6

would stand, but there was a problem. Relentless hoards kept replacing those he felled and the sun was going down too fast for him to complete the job. So he spoke to the **sun**. It was there by God's word, therefore it could respond to a word. Be it Joshua's or God's word, the sun obeyed. It stood still.

Jesus spoke to **sicknesses** and they went. He spoke to **demons** and they went. He taught his disciples to do the same. He spoke to **waves** and they calmed. This story (Mt 8) begins and ends with a rebuke. He rebuked the disciples for their lack of faith when they woke Him for help, fearing the boat was sinking. Then He rebuked the **sea** and it calmed. He was addressing two things: fear was to be no longer part of their lives; and they, like He, had authority over the storm. Why call Him?

All of these things were in some way a problem, misalignment to God's divine order. He was re-establishing His Father's Dominion again on earth.

He spoke to a fig **tree** and it died. He spoke to **dead bodies** and they lived. He commanded **fish** to do all sorts of things – to swarm into Zebedee's nets (the fishermen's fruitless night was a problem); to produce a coin for the tax man (not to pay him was definitely a problem); (and in His pre-flesh days) to swallow, rescue and transport Jonah to where he ought to be (Jonah's disobedience was a problem).

Jesus spoke to animate and inanimate things. He created everything with a word; therefore everything can hear Him. He can command everything. It's interesting that Satan's first temptation for Jesus was to use the power of His word for a selfish reason.[61] *"Command these stones to become bread.* Poor you, you're so hungry. You need food now for strength to launch Your ministry. We know Your words have power to create." But Jesus knew better; the angels came and ministered to Him. And very soon after that He was in Cana performing His first miracle and launching His ministry by creating an over-abundance of wine for a wedding celebration.[62]

---

61   Lk 4:1–13; Mt 4:1–11
62   Jn 2:1–12

There were Old Testament characters who captured this principle and spoke to nature. Elijah commanded **rain** to stop for three years and then to start again. He commanded **fire** from heaven. (God commanded **ravens** for him so he could survive the drought he'd caused.) James notes that Elijah was *'a man just like us'*. (Jas 5:18)

Moses parted the Red **Sea**. Later he had opposition in his camp and he told the people, *"This is how you'll know that it was God… it wasn't anything I cooked up on my own… If the ground opens up and swallows them… The words were hardly out of his mouth when the earth split open. Earth opened its mouth and in one gulp swallowed down Korah and his family.* (Num 16:33) **Earth** responded to Moses' words.

Jesus, after speaking to the fig tree, said to his disciples, "You can do stuff like this. In fact you can *tell this mountain, 'Move!' and it would move.*" (Mat 17:20) When I was a teenager and just learning to see visions I saw a mountain with tiny bulldozers working hard to cut away a little slice of a mountain. It was an impossible task to remove the whole mountain. Suddenly it began to topple and the whole thing fell over. "I saw it, I saw it!" I began shouting. "I saw the mountain fall into the sea!" I was so excited; I knew it could happen. *Nothing will be impossible for you.* (Mat 17:20NKJV)

Droughts break, walls collapse (Berlin), rulers topple (Saddam Hussein), at the word of His servants. William Branham stopped bulls and hornets; he spoke to animals and they did his bidding. We are given authority to bid and forbid, to allow and disallow, to bind and to loose.

God spoke: *"Let us make human beings in our image, make them reflecting our nature so they can be responsible for the fish in the sea, the birds in the air, the cattle, and yes, Earth itself, and every animal that moves on the face of the earth."* (Gen 1:26-28)

Hebrews says, *You put them in charge of your entire handcrafted world.*[63]

---

63   Heb 2:5-10 When God put them in charge of everything, nothing was excluded. But we don't see it yet, don't see everything under human jurisdiction.

So we, His Regents, are responsible for the welfare of everything in His dominion. What we speak must be aligned to the order He has designed for His creation. He has paid an exorbitant price to rectify Adam's mistake. He is now depending on us to re-establish His order in every corner of the planet. Earth is groaning for the Sons of God to appear.[64] Jesus put it this way: *Thy Kingdom come, Thy will be done on Earth as it is Heaven.* (Mat 6:10KJV)

~

---

[64] Rom 8:19;21

Chapter 10

"Learn To Do Authority Like Jesus Did"

As I woke this morning to work on 'your Juris in your jurisdiction' – about what's spiritually legal and what's not, I heard clearly in my spirit the words, "Learn to do authority like Jesus did". God interjected this instruction as I write to you. They are His direct words for you and for me – "In learning to do authority, do it like Jesus did".

So, obediently, I'm taking you on a walk to examine how He did it. Jesus was a heap of fun, radically different.[65]

Kingdom Focus

All His life here on planet earth Jesus never lost focus. He had come from Heaven, a spirit Being, and was now housed in a finite body like us, but His spirit lived in God's spirit realm no matter where He was on earth. He never lost sight of Who He was: God's Son, King of Heaven (even though He'd laid aside the

> *You put him [The Son] in charge of everything human so he might give real and eternal life to all in his charge.*
> John 17:2

---

65 I love the video (movie) The Gospel According to St John

role for the time). He never lost sight of His purpose: to conquer death and make a Door for us into God's kingdom and a door for Heaven to planet earth, re-establishing the connection between Heaven and earth. His focus, then, was:

- What He was
- Who He was
- What He was here for

This intense focus was obvious when He was twelve years old.[66] His parents lost him (He wasn't lost!), ostensibly in the crowds returning from the Jerusalem feast. But in fact He hadn't left the Temple. When, beside themselves with worry after a frantic three days, they found Him, He said, *"Didn't you understand I'd have to be engaging in My Father's business?"* (v. 49)

I love the way He persistently talked from a heavenly perspective, out of the invisible eternal kingdom where His spirit lived. That's my goal. This morning depicts how short I fall of it. God often has to catch me just as I'm waking to make sure He gets heard, before my mind 'takes charge' and the things of the day get under way. Mostly the day's noise and clutter increasingly siphon my attention off my spirit man (vertical focus), and drop my attention to the clamour of earthly things (horizontal focus). "Walk in the Spirit," Jesus instructs us.

He did it so well. He said wild things quite incomprehensible to literal thinkers who were stuck in their earthly mindsets. "You need to be born again, Nicodemus – die to your old religious patterns and be born into My spirit kingdom."

To the woman at the well, "If you understood the spirit realm you'd ask Me for water. My water will quench your thirst forever."[67]

"You haven't anything to draw with," she answered from down here.

---

66 Lk 2:41-45

67 John 4. Throughout this chapter I will be paraphrasing stories from John's Gospel. All direct quotes (italics) from John's Gospel in this chapter are from NKJV unless otherwise noted. Read through all the red-letter Jesus words in John for an exhilarating exercise. John was very alert to this Spirit dimension.

"My living water will be a spring gushing out of you." Jesus time and again refused to be pulled down into earthly perspectives. "This is nothing to do with buckets, Girl, I'm talking to your very thirsty spirit being."

An hilarious picture of this spirit versus rational divide is painted in John 8. The religious leaders are at Him again, and in course of the dialogue Jesus states that Abraham looked ahead and delighted to see His day. I love His perspective. Constantly focussed in the spirit realm, He is aware of the total panorama of history and the significance of this moment.

"You!" they guffaw. "How old are you? And you've seen Abraham?!" That's not even what Jesus had said, but He ignores it and responds: "Indeed, before Abraham was, I AM." Their spirits need to know that a greater than Abraham is here. They grab up rocks to stone Him and He disappears. Worse than body/spirit disconnect, or even criminal neglect, these Pharisees are guilty of abuse – "No, my caged spirit, you are not going to feed from this man".

Knowing Who He Was

Jesus knew unshakably Who He was, and was not backward in voicing it. He had the unchallengeable legal position of being God – His 'juris'; and He freely spoke it – His 'diction'. He understood that His jurisdiction included 'everything human', including these human spirits which He wanted to bring alive.

"I am the Bread of Life, sent down from Heaven. If you eat this bread you will live forever. My words are spirit words; they give life. Does this offend you?" Many left Him at that stage,[68] their earthly bodies carrying their hungry spirits away, refusing food to their most important component. Jesus was concerned about their spirits, the eternal part of them. *We do not look at the things that are seen, but the things that are not seen. For the things that are seen are temporal, but the things that are not seen are eternal.* (2 Cor 4:18 NKJV) Since everything

---

68   This paraphrase from Ch.5

we can see and touch around us will eventually be destroyed, surely its relevance dims compared with the significance of ever lasting things.

"This Temple will be demolished, but in three days it will rise again," He said. He Himself was now the Temple of God on earth. He was the place where God lived and interacted with His people. Was He pronouncing 'Ichabod' ('The glory has departed') on Solomon's glorious temple?

"Who do you think you are? By what authority do you do these things? We are the Sanhedrin. We are the rulers and spiritual leaders. It didn't come from us!" They recognized some kind of authority here, what was it? It was something beyond them. Must be Beelzebub![69]

"My Father, Who sent Me, tells Me what to say and how to say it. I'm under His authority; He gives the command."[70] *"I do not speak on My own authority, but the Father who dwells in Me does the works."*(Jn 14:10)

So, the works and the words were specifically on the authority of 'One Who sent Him' – a spiritual authority higher than theirs. *You are from beneath; I am from above. You are of this world; I am not of this world.* (Jn 8:23NKJV) No wonder they were challenged and upset!

Not only the religious leaders noticed his authority; the common people did too. "This is just the carpenter's son, where did He get all this knowledge?"

But if the religious leaders and the people didn't know who He was, the spirit world did. Jesus' Spirit was totally visible to them and they knew Who He was. Spirits see in the spirit realm. We can't because, until we have connected with His living Spirit, our spirit is dead. *You have no life in you.* (Jn 6:53)

Evil spirits recognized Him and His authority. As soon as He arrived in Gadarene territory a legion of spirits confronted him. "Hey Jesus, Son of God, why are you coming to our territory, bothering us? … No, no, if you cast us out, don't send us to the fire yet! Let us go into the pigs." They knew they were illegally occupying the man and

---

69   Prince of demons or Satan.
70   Jn 12

Jesus would evict them, that He was the rightful owner. They also acknowledged that they knew their ultimate destiny.[71]

Paul did authority like Jesus did and he experienced a similar story. A girl inhabited by a fortune-telling spirit followed his party about, loudly proclaiming what the spirit recognized: *"These men are servants of the Most High God. They are telling you the way to be saved!"* (Acts 16:16-18 NKJV) After three days Paul was exasperated and cast out the spirit in the Name of Jesus. It obeyed him – leaving the girl's owner without his income. (Come to think of it, the swineherds lost their income too. Jesus delivers those oppressed by evil spirits with no consideration for those who gain their living from sin. He's not politically correct that way.)

Making Right Judgments

Judgment was part of Jesus' jurisdictional mandate. *The Father has given the Son authority to execute judgment because He is the Son of Man ... I can of Myself do nothing. As I hear I judge, and my judgment is righteous because I do not seek my own will.* (Jn 5:27; 30) Jesus' holiness was a plumb line; it measured what was right and what was wrong. "How dare you make My Father's house a den of thieves?" He drove out the money-makers with a little rope whip, cleansing the Temple.

Testing Him, self-righteous men brought a woman 'caught in the act'. (Aren't there two actors in this 'act'?) "The law says she should be stoned. What do you say, Teacher?" You can hear the smarm. "Let whoever's sinless cast the first stone," and Jesus began making a sin list in the dust. They slunk away one by one. "Where are your accusers?" He asked at last. "Hasn't anyone condemned you? ... No? Neither do I. Go and sin no more."

He healed a cripple at Bethesda and said the same, "Go and sin no more – in case you get something worse."

---

71 This story is found in Mt 8; Mk 5; Lk 8.

Then his disciples came with a question: "Lord, who sinned, this blind man or his parents?" Jesus laid that assumption to rest. "Neither this man nor his parents sinned, but so you'd see an example of God's glory."[72] Sickness may be, but is not always the direct result of sin. It may be just waiting for a Son of God to manifest His glory.

Leading By Example

John the Baptist had pointed Jesus out to the crowds. "There's the One I told you would come. He's so far greater than me, that I wouldn't even presume, as His lowliest servant, to kneel and undo His sandals."

But Jesus joined the queue for baptism. "No way! This is the wrong way round. I'm the one who needs to be baptised by You!" John protested.

But Jesus insisted. *"It is proper for us to do this to fulfil all righteousness.* (Mt 3:15 NIV) *"Do it. God's work, putting things right all these centuries, is coming together right now in this baptism."* (Msg. version)

And the moment He rose from the water Father, Son and Holy Spirit came together –

>Son: a Man under authority
>Holy Spirit: visible as a dove
>Father: audible – all giving witness to this pivotal moment.

A lot of Jesus' teaching was by example. If these followers were disciples they would be learning, and expected to do as their Master did. Hence the fiasco when Jesus came down from the Mount of Transfiguration and the disciples hadn't been able to cast out the epileptic spirit. Everyone expected it.

When Jesus arrived He exclaimed, *"What a generation! No sense of God! No focus to your lives! How many times do I have to go over these things?"* He rebuked the epileptic spirit and it went.

The disciples asked Him privately, "How come we couldn't do it?"

"Because you're not yet taking God seriously," Jesus said. "The simple

---

72   John chapters 2; 8; 5; 9

truth is that if you had a mere kernel of faith...there is nothing you wouldn't be able to tackle." (Mt 17:14-20)

"In fact, if you're really my disciples you will do what I do, *and greater works than these you will do because I go to My Father.*" (Jn 14:12)

"I commission you to go out and make disciples," He told them, "*Instruct them in the practice of all I have commanded you.*" (Mt 28:20) "*I have given you an example that you should do as I have done to you.*" (Jn 13:17) So we do what He does as an example to others, and they show others ... and so it multiplies.

I hope, if there was ever any doubt, this convinces you of your mandate. Whatever He did, we do. And He makes sure we know how by His constant example.

Paul gives a revealing insight into how example works. He says to the Thessalonians: ... *you became imitators of us and of the Lord; in spite of severe suffering you welcomed the message with joy ... and so you became a model to all the believers in Macedonia.* (1Thess 1:5 NIV)

The Lord < Paul < Thessalonians < Macedonians < others – and so it spreads.

Not Seeking His Own Will

"*I came to do the will of Him Who sent me,*" Jesus said. We all totally sympathise with those excruciating moments when it comes to the final crunch and He goes back over the contract – "Isn't there any other way? Up to now I've done everything You asked Me, Father. And I've shepherded and prepared these You gave me, haven't lost one. Isn't this enough?

> There is no such thing as God's Work without Him; it is merely our own.

Do I have to go through with this last horrendous task? *Never-the-less* (interesting word compound – He will never take the lesser way), *not My will, but Yours.*" Is this Jesus' first ever Me-focussed prayer? But **we** won out – not for Himself, but for us because the Father willed to redeem us.

I learned a powerful lesson from Pacific Islands prophet, Michael Maeliau. We were chatting about a significant global conference we had just attended. "The war is over," said Michael. "There are just a few last skirmishes on the way." A long silence full of my questions ensued, until he summed it up. "But God can't do what He wants to do until men stop building their own kingdoms."

There is the crux and the tragedy of it all. *"I do not seek my own glory,"* Jesus said. (Jn 8:50) It's so very hard for us to get out of the way.

Psychology's 'Recovery Philosophy' (Consumer-Centred) has an interesting maxim:
'Nothing about us without us.'

'Without Him I can do nothing.' There is no such thing as 'God's work' without Him; it is merely our own.

~

Chapter 11
Your Juris In Your Jurisdiction

Prophet Michael was right. So often our focus slips and things become about us instead of God, about our kingdom instead of His. This hinders God from achieving His agendas. 'Human rights', especially His Own, wasn't big on Jesus' agenda.

In this chapter I want to discuss some issues with rights and boundaries. 'Juris' is the legal part of Jurisdiction – juris = law; diction = speak. So, as we've learned, your jurisdiction is the area over which you have legal right to speak. In other words: the sphere of influence God has given you over which to establish His dominion.

Definition

Governing an earthly jurisdiction is about interpreting and applying the law, legislating, administering justice, making pronouncements on legal matters. It also has defined areas of responsibility.[73]

God has commissioned you to your spiritual jurisdiction. "*He determined the times set for them and the exact places where they should live.*" (Acts 17:26 NIV) God is saying: rule that jurisdiction the way Jesus did.

So let's take a look at laws in this invisible kingdom we're ruling – this

---

[73] West's Encyclopedia of American Law

heaven on earth we're establishing. How much control do we have with this mandate to rule? Is this heaven for the 'control freak'?

Sorry, even though it's your jurisdiction, it's not your dominion you're establishing. As we've said before, it's not people we are ruling, but the spirit realm that affects them. You have all the authority and backing of Heaven, nothing is impossible to you, but it's all about Him. Of Him, by Him, for Him are all things.

An Upside-down Kingdom

This spiritual kingdom is certainly an upside-down sovereignty. Humility sits on the throne and rules with a rod of Love. In this kingdom we live by faith and not by sight. Jesus said it was the 'poor in spirit' who would inherit it.[74] And, as He prepared them for His departure, Jesus gave His disciples a 'new commandment' (rule) – to love one another. Love fulfils all the law. And there is no slave-master, Fear, cracking whips. It's all about loving Him because He first loved us, and serving Him because it's our greatest joy.

So What Are The Rules?

What law is it that we 'interpret and apply'? Ten Commandments, Old Testament laws? Wait. Didn't *'the law of the Spirit',* make us *'free from the law'* (Rom 8:2 NKJV) which was about sin, and death? The law of the Spirit is about Life. *If you are led by the Spirit, you are not under law.* (Gal 5:17)

Obvious when you think about it! The Spirit is God. He has ultimate, invincible authority. (See the story of the Paraclete controlling my horse in the next chapter.) He is now in us and we are operating under His instructions. How then can laws apply to the Highest Authority Who set everything in order and running in the first place? He is ultimate Love, Goodness, Rightness, Holiness, Justice, etc. He's above law. That doesn't put us above the law; it means if we are led by Him no law applies to us. *The entire law is*

---

74 Jas 2:5; Mt 5:3

summed up in one single command: "Love your neighbour as yourself."[75]

So in learning to do authority (ruling, governing), like Jesus did as He introduced this Kingdom, let's follow Him by checking ourselves against the headings of the last chapter. We saw our Master was undistractedly focussed, knowing:

1. What He was,
2. Who He was, and
3. What He was here for.

Then we watched Him walk that out in His day-to-day life.

Know What You Are

You too are a spirit housed in a temporal body. The earthly casing will drop away one day (or may be transformed in the blink of an eye!) and you will be left the real you, the important part who lasts forever. It is vitally important that we give quality attention to this 'spirit man' who is our true self. He needs food and drink and bathing and clothing[76] – the basic essentials of life. He doesn't demand you spend thousands on food, toiletries, cosmetics, and fashions like you may do on his decaying container! Everything he needs is at the one Source, Christ. No shopping around! He is allergic to merchandise from any other provider! (Your spirit will die from those toxins and the rot will provide a place for demons to infest.)

> Your spirit is allergic to merchandise from any other Provider.

Know Who You Are

To everyone who believed Jesus, He gave the right (juris) to become children of God. The Message puts it this way: *Whoever believed he was who he claimed and would do what he said, he made to be their true selves, their child-of-God selves. These are the God-begotten.* (Jn 1:12)

Paul talks about how you know this: *God's Spirit touches our spirits*

---

75 Gal 3:24; 5:6,14 NIV
76 Jn 6:55; Eph 5:26; Rev 3:18

and confirms who we really are. We know who he is, and we know who we are: Father and children. (Rom 8:16, 17)

Growing up as little girl in an antagonistic culture, my daughter had a 'secret weapon'. *You are of God, little children, and have overcome them, because He that is in you is greater than He that is in the world.* (1 Jn 4:4NKJV) Not everyone listened to Jesus, and not everyone will listen to you, He warns. Spirits that won't admit Jesus is 'God come in the flesh' are of the spirit of antichrist. Don't worry about them. Knowing who you are and Who lives in you drives out fear.

The Lion

> I looked out of my glass doors and there he was lying on my lawn in the rays of the setting sun, his coat all glowing golden. He sat up, tipped back his head and roared. First came the g-g-g-g-guttural prelude like a huge engine starting up. Then the voice cut in. The sound reverberated around the hills and valleys. Everything stopped. Nature held its breath. All of creation recognized Who this was. Then unbelievably He padded over to me, stood on His hind legs, reached His huge paws over my shoulders and enveloped me in the most enormous hug. I was His and He was mine. I knew it. I was overwhelmed to be shown a love like this! [77]

He appears again on occasion. Once He seemed to be pacing restlessly out there on my lawn. My brain said, "That can't be the Lion of the Tribe of Judah; God doesn't get agitated". In my spirit I walked out towards Him. He grabbed me in under Him and I could feel the guttural growling in His throat as He gazed towards the gate. Never have I felt so safe. I knew He would defend me to the hilt against anything. I was His and He was mine. That's who I am. And I have a Defender, a new experience!

---

[77] This experience happened in an open-eyed vision. I came upon this video later on which depicts exactly what it was like – minus the cage. Watch it, you'll be blessed.
Video: <http://www.vitality101.com/Fun/lion-kisses-rescuer>

Know Your Authority

Jesus said, *All authority has been given to me in heaven and in earth; go therefore and do all I commanded you... and I'll be with you – always – even to the end of the Age.* (Mt 28:18-20 NKJV) (That's not far off in my reckoning. Not much daylight left in which to work.)

The person who trusts in me will not only do what I've been doing but even greater things, because I, on my way to the Father, am giving you the same work to do that I've been doing. You can count on it. From now on, whatever you request along the lines of who I am and what I am doing, I'll do it. (Jn 14:12)

You have power to kick out the evil spirits, bring health to the sick, raise the dead, and generally establish the climate of the kingdom where you are.[78] **Our standing in the world is identical with Christ's.** (1 Jn 4:17) (*As He is so are we in the world.* NKJV) That's pretty revolutionary to our confidence!

And *this honour have all His saints* – to carry out the judgment written against spiritual kings and rulers, to bind them in chains and fetters of iron. (Ps 149)

Here's an Old Testament example from the physical Promised Land. Joshua received this word: *God has driven out superpower nations before you. And up to now, no one has been able to stand up to you. Think of it – one of you single-handedly, putting a thousand on the run! Because God is God, your God. Because he fights for you, just as he promised.* (Josh 23:9)

Know Your Purpose

For this purpose the Son of God was manifested that He might destroy the works of the devil. (1 Jn 3:8) That is: evil. In His inaugural preach Jesus quoted Isaiah 61 listing all the things He came to do – bring healing and deliverance and freedom and joy ... all of which activities destroy Satan's works.

As a disciple of the Lord, and an heir of the Kingdom, you too have been sent to announce, "The Kingdom of Heaven is here!" (Tara tara!

---

78 Concepts from Mat 10

Blow the trumpets!) and to establish that kingdom on earth.

Paul often reiterated his purpose. God told him, *I'm sending you to open the eyes of the outsiders so they can see the difference between dark and light, and choose light, see the difference between Satan and God, and choose God ... to present my offer of sins forgiven, and a place in the family.* (Acts 26:17) Paul said, *This is my life work; helping people to understand and respond to this message ... the inexhaustible riches and generosity of Christ.* (Eph 3:7)
Paul tells the Ephesians he *continually asks God*
> *to make you intelligent*
> *and discerning in*
> *knowing him personally,*
> *your eyes focused and clear,*
> *so that you can see exactly what it is he is calling you to do ...*
> *grasp the utter extravagance of his work in us who trust him –*
> *endless energy,*
> *boundless strength!*

All this energy issues from Christ; God raised him from death and set him on a throne in deep heaven, in charge of running the universe ... no name and no power exempt from his rule ... He is in charge of it all, has the final word on everything.[79] *At the centre of all this Christ rules the church ... The church is Christ's body in which he speaks and acts.* (Eph 1:16-23)

When Solomon was about to take over his father's kingdom David pronounced a special blessing over his son, which can apply to us from our Father today: *God speed as you build the sanctuary for your God, the job God has given you... Courage! Take charge! Don't be timid; don't hold back ... look at all I've provided for you.* (1 Chr 22:11-14)

Both David and Paul go on to request resources for their sons to carry out the tasks – discernment, understanding, reverent obedience, clear-centred focus – then they declare that all that their offspring need is lavishly supplied.

What He's calling us to do is extravagantly huge, infinitely significant.

---

79 Remind you of Joseph?

Christ is the Source and Centre, all the energy and resources are inexhaustible. He runs absolutely everything, 'no name or power exempt', and He does it through His body. Did you get that that's you? That's huge!

Not Seeking His Own Will

In knowing His purpose Jesus didn't self-serve; He did only what His Father planned. In other words He ruled as a man under authority.

Look at Jeremiah's commissioning. *Say exactly what I tell you to say. Don't pull your punches ... I'm making you as impregnable as a castle, immovable as a steel post, solid as a concrete block wall. You're a one-man defence system against this culture. They'll fight you, but they won't even scratch you. I'll back you up every inch of the way.* (Jer 1:17ff) That's a very comforting promise, to be backed up by God. But of course, if we're only being obedient, it's His responsibility. We're under authority.

Know Your Boundaries

There are borders to our jurisdictions. Jesus had none (except that He was confined to one human body), but we do, because His Kingdom is portioned out to His regents. King David, the man after God's heart, whose kingdom mirrored God's kingdom design, allocated jurisdictions for his people. They were spheres of responsibility, sometimes geographic and sometimes task-oriented.

For example, Kenaniah's family were to be officials and judges, but their jurisdiction did not extend to worship and the sanctuary (which was the Levites' responsibility). Both 1 & 11 Chronicles list the people's allocated jurisdictions. It was obviously important to David. He pointed out his role in contrast to Joab's in restoring the city. He also pointed out 'my part and your part' to Solomon. *My part in this* (his accession) *was to put down the enemies, subdue the land to God and his people;* **your** *part is to give yourselves heart and soul to praying to your God. So get moving, build the house of worship.* (1 Chr 22:16)

Each of our jurisdictions is crucial to getting the work done and building God's Kingdom on earth. We are each responsible for the part allocated to us.

What God tells you to do is within your boundary. He has included it in your jurisdiction. It may surprise you, you may feel it's far beyond you, but if it's God He will enable and provide for you to do it. Don't be put off if others are shocked and say, "Who do you think you are?" Satan will happily challenge you in this way. Just make sure you have heard correctly from God, and obey God despite man. It is before God you ultimately stand or fall.

I remember when God spoke to me to go to the Himalayas. It was way outside what I considered my jurisdiction and outside of any areas I was familiar with. I protested, "Lord, didn't you notice I'm a woman? And I'm sixty! … And who in the world would come with me anyway?" "Bill from NZ," said God. And sure enough Bill was the first to sign up for the team.

On the other hand, what He doesn't tell you to do is likely outside your jurisdiction. Check it out with Him.

Overlapping Boundaries

You may find that your boundaries overlap. If you find that what God seems to be telling you to do, others are doing or have done, don't worry about it. Think about all the people God told to go to the Berlin Wall and command it to come down. There are numbers of such stories of obedience. Who knows when enough is enough? My teenage daughter once said to me, "Mum, how do you know if **your** prayer isn't the last one to fill the bowl and tip it over?" That thought impacted her to keep praying even when the situation seemed intransigent – and encouraged me no end.

An Example of Overlap

The story of Peter's first visit to the Gentiles is an interesting comment on overlapping jurisdictions. Cornelius was an Italian Centurion serving under Rome in the city of Caesarea. He was a very devout man and favoured by Jews and God. One day, while he was fasting, this seasoned soldier was startled by the appearance of an angel coming in and addressing him by name. The angel first diplomatically commended his character, then commanded him to send men to the Jewish seaport of Joppa. So he did – a man not just under Roman authority, but God's Kingdom authority, which took precedence. He sent two trusted servants and a God-fearing soldier.

Meanwhile Peter has received his sheet-of-meat vision and told to eat, as nothing God cleansed was to be rejected. "Three men are at the door, get up and go with them," a voice says. So Peter receives the invitation to Caesarea to visit the Gentile Italian. This is highly irregular. However in obedience to the vision he sets out next day with the visitors, plus a handful of Jewish believers.

By the end of the day they arrive at the centurion's house to find Cornelius has invited his whole platoon and his friends, not to mention the extended family. The centurion prostrates himself at Peter's feet. "No, no! I'm just a man. Get up!" Woops, boundaries are not yet clear here. Peter enters, explaining (not so diplomatically) how unlawful it is for him to be here – except for the vision. "So why have you called me?"

"We're all here before God to hear what He wants to say through you." (Cornelius is quite clear about the purpose.) So Peter preaches Jesus: "We witnessed it all …" He's nowhere near finished speaking when the Holy Spirit interrupts by falling on everyone. To his astonishment, these Gentiles are speaking in tongues and experiencing a Pentecost just like had happened to him and Jesus' disciples.

So he commanded them to be baptised. Here is a fisherman taking charge in the house of the Italian centurion, commanding this commander and his platoon and his house-guests. He took initiative in the jurisdiction God had brought him into and it was not presumption.

There are hierarchies of jurisdictions. Peter's was a spiritual one; Cornelius' was a military one. Other examples are Peter in prison after the earthquake telling the jailer what to do, and Paul, a prisoner, taking charge on the sinking ship. The authority they had in God superseded earthly authorities.

Respecting Boundaries

Paul has a revealing piece of writing about jurisdictional boundaries. Paul's converts in Corinth are receiving teaching from someone else and no longer want to receive instruction from Paul. He's 'overstepping the mark' they've been saying. Paul responds. *We aren't making outrageous claims here. We're sticking to the limits of what God has for us. But there can be no question that those limits reach to and include you. We're not moving into someone else's "territory". We were already there with you. We were the first ones to get there with the message of Christ, right? So how can there be any question about our overstepping our bounds by writing or visiting you? We're not barging in on the rightful work of others, interfering with their ministries.*

Paul gave birth to these spiritual children; they would always be within his jurisdiction no matter where they were or with whom, because they would never cease to be his children. He also respects the ministries and jurisdictions of others stating that he has no intention of moving in on what others have done, or taking credit for it. He just wants them all to play a part in expanding the work '*and we'll all be within the limits God sets as we proclaim the Message in countries beyond Corinth*'. (2 Cor 10:12-18)

Overstepping the Boundary

Uzziah was a good king influenced by his godly father and the prophet Zechariah. God blessed him with many victories as he drove out Judah's enemies. But he pushed divine favour too far when he stepped out of his jurisdiction to burn incense to the Lord in the temple. Eighty brave priests confronted him. "You have overstepped your rights, your majesty. Only consecrated sons of Aaron may perform this task. You must 'stop trespassing' and leave." Uzziah pointed an angry arm at their temerity in opposing the king. God struck him immediately with leprosy – from which he suffered until his death.[80] An ignominious end to an otherwise great reign.

---

[80] 2 Chr 26

Note, God supported the spiritual custodians (priests) against the civic ruler (king).

Boundaries and Judgments

Here is an issue that troubles me. I believe heartily in intercession, in standing in the gap, in identificational repentance, and I know we can stay God's hand of judgment, stop destructive storms, turn political tides – nothing is impossible. But as Paul says, *Just because something is technically legal doesn't mean that it's spiritually appropriate.* (1 Cor 6:12) What we intercede for may not always be in God's or our best interests.

God with a couple of angels visited His friend Abraham. *"The cries of the victims in Sodom and Gomorrah are deafening; the sin of those cities is immense."* (Gen.18:20) "I am about to deal with it," He said. The angels walked on, but Abraham stood in front of the Lord and blocked His way. "You can't do this, promise me. There might be some righteous people ..." We know the bargaining story. In the end there weren't ten righteous people in those cities. But God knew Abraham's intercession was really for his nephew, Lot. So God answered his heart cry and the two angels physically dragged the family of four out of Sodom by their arms. Lot's wife didn't make it; just Dad and the girls, still arguing about going. But when they saw the destruction they were happy enough to get up into the hills where they were told.

Isolated, all their companions cinders on the plains, the girls took the initiative to keep their father's line alive and produce offspring to their father. The two resultant sons became the Moabites and the Ammonites, long-time enemies of God's people until now. (Today geographic Jordan.) So, could Abraham's intercessory compassion actually have been inappropriate and presumptuous? Was it motivated out of his heart, but not God's? We know God often gives what we ask, even when it is not what He desires. We then bear the consequences.

So, are our many intercessions for God to stay His hand of judgment actually beneficial, or are they ultimately making things worse? He required the Israelites to totally eradicate their enemies, to cleanse the land of idolatry and sin and heal the land. *It was God's idea that they (the nations of the Promised Land) would stubbornly fight the Israelites so He could put them under a holy curse without mercy. That way He could destroy them.* (Josh 11:20) God's judgments are in fact merciful, getting rid of the evil so it cannot increase and enslave even more victims. His holy Kingdom cannot be built over sin.

Rather than presumptuously prevent catastrophes (*lest you even be found to fight against God.* [Acts 5:39 NKJV]) perhaps our prayers should be that, in the troubles, people be brought to cry out to God and have a true encounter with Him and His mercy. *Everyone who calls, "Help, God!" gets help.* (Rom 10:13)

Are Calamities God's Judgments?

It is currently a popular teaching that God does not cause or use calamities to bring judgment or punishment for sin, and that prophets who prophesy judgments are false prophets. (This judgment has been hurtful to those called to the true role of Prophet.) I understand the motivation is to correct an image of a vengeful God, replacing Him with a God of Love. But the two images are not mutually exclusive. It is His love that keeps on warning us that sin will lead to destruction. Sin ultimately brings its own consequences because it is out of harmony with God's creation and ways, and produces chaos.

The favourite scripture of pray-ers, (2Chron 7:14) *if my people will humble themselves and pray,* is preceded by this alert (v.13): *When I shut up the heavens and there is no rain, or command the locusts to devour the land, or send pestilence among My people...* In v.14 He refers to the reason for the calamities being their 'wicked ways' and their 'sin'. He makes it clear that the purpose for the calamities is to turn the people to repentance so He can forgive, and heal.

I will come near you for judgment. I will be a swift witness against sorcerers, against adulterers, against perjurers, against those who exploit wage-earners and widows and orphans, and against those who turn away an alien, because they do not fear me. (Mal 3:5)

He talks of using pestilence and bloodshed, flooding rain, great hailstones, fire and brimstone. *Thus I will magnify Myself and I will be known in the eyes of many nations.* (Ez 38:22) His heart cry is that they may acknowledge Me.

The prophet Nahum tells us: *The Lord is slow to anger and great in power. And He will not at all acquit the wicked. The Lord has His way in the whirlwind and in the storm and the clouds are the dust of His feet… The mountains quake before Him, the hills melt, and the earth heaves at His presence…The Lord is good. A stronghold in the day of trouble. And He knows those who trust in Him.* (Nah 1:3-7)

The Lord is known by the judgment He executes. (Ps 9:16)

You need New Testament examples? Didn't Jesus take all the punishment for sin? Let's look at the very start of the Church.

The followers of the Way are selling off whatever land and goods are superfluous to their new lifestyle and sharing it with those who have little. Ananias and Sapphira are caught up in the fervour. Their donation will look good in the eyes of the apostles and the believers. The sale of their holiday house brought in $300,000 they'll say. They'll keep $50,000, nice little buffer. After all, none of this is compulsory.

Ananias makes the presentation to Peter. "So the house sold for $300,000?" "Yes Brother Peter, God is so good."

"How can you imagine you can lie to the HOLY Ghost and He wouldn't know? You could have kept the lot; no one asked you for it. But you let Satan pervert your heart and you lied to God." Ananias drops dead on the spot.

Sapphira hasn't got word yet. She arrives – maybe to see what's taking her husband so long. "So Sapphira, tell me how much you sold the land for." "Oh Brother Peter, $300,000. Isn't God good!"

"So both of you made this little conspiracy to lie to the HOLY Ghost. The young men who buried your husband will be here any minute. They'll bury you beside him."

This is a Holy God we're representing and His Body, His spiritual temple, is required to be holy. This shock beginning to the Church parallels the inauguration of the Tabernacle – the physical place set up for God to live in. Aaron's two sons, on the first day, substituted their own fire in place of God's.

They too were struck dead instantly.

God is still Judge, He set the standard at the beginning. But His compassion continually tries to get our attention and warn us.

At the time of the 'first' Christchurch earthquake, Sept 2010, my spirit trembled at the name, 'Christ's church'. He had said He would shake His church. Was this a very visible warning of what was to happen in the spiritual?

In following the news I heard the mayor describing the quake which was 7.1 on the Richter scale. He was thankful that despite considerable damage there was no direct loss of life. "We're used to earthquakes, but the most remarkable thing about this one was the violence of it." As he said this I heard the Lord's voice say clearly: "If this shaking doesn't get your attention and bring repentance I will have to be even more violent. I want my Church back." Six months later there was another quake, only 6.3 on the Richter scale, but 185 people died.

I don't believe Christchurch was any more sinful than any other city, or especially those unfortunate enough to have been victims. I do believe the Judge calls out through such events – "Please take heed, return to Me, I am the only One Who can save you. Catastrophic events are increasing, and the End is getting close. Come back to Me." (Compare Ninevah.)

Other Juris Issues

Initiative versus Presumption

During my teens I was troubled by this question. How could I be sure I wasn't being presumptuous? Satan used this fear to hold me back from stepping out and doing things God was prompting me to. I was afraid of being presumptuous and displeasing Him.

I didn't yet comprehend the Love of the Father, nor that He often places desires in our hearts specifically because He wants to grant those desires. (Ps 37:4) God delights in the little stumbling steps His children take in following Him. He doesn't reprimand us for falling. He picks us up and encourages us to learn from the spills. Like our Father, we are creative beings. He has given us the ability to grasp opportunities, to respond creatively, to initiate. After all He is the Alpha, the Beginning One living through us.

Initiative

One of my favourite Bible stories about initiative is Abigail's. She was the battered wife of a bad-tempered abusive husband. He was wealthy and mean. She heard Nabal had refused supplies to David's troops who were taking refuge in the area, and that a contingent of David's army was on its way in revenge. Abigail took bold initiative. She had her servants prepare all kinds of food and supplies, loaded them on donkeys and headed out to meet the soldiers.

Bowing humbly before David she asked forgiveness on behalf of her surly husband, and offered the gifts she had brought. "If you hadn't stepped in," David said, "I swear your husband and his property would all be destroyed by tomorrow." Abigail even took the initiative to prophesy to the future king of Israel and encourage him. You know the sequel: God killed Nabal with a heart attack and Abigail later became Mrs David. (1 Sam 25)

An old lady took initiative and stopped a bloodbath. Joab, King David's military commander, had set up a siege around a city in Israel.

The old lady, instead of cowering inside, came onto the wall and called for Joab. "*Why are you messing with God's legacy like this, tearing down one of Israel's mother cities?*" she challenged. "No, no I'm not out to destroy, but Sheba has revolted against the King and half Israel with him. He's hiding here. If you hand him over we'll be gone."

"His head will be thrown to you from the wall," she promised. She presented her strategy to the city elders and they did what she said. Joab blew the ram's horn and the soldiers went home. Israel was reunited. (2 Sam 20)

There are wonderful stories of initiative taken by unexpected people, who step up and save the day, speak words of strategic wisdom, win amazing victories. King Josiah of Judah destroyed the high places, cleansing all Judah of idolatry and went on to do the same in his neighbour Israel's territory – zealous for God's holiness. Jonathan and his armour-bearer snatched an opportunity and defeated an attacking army by themselves.[81]

These were fighting for a physical kingdom; we on this side of the Cross war for a spiritual one. Their stories were recorded as examples for us, to encourage and warn us.[82]

Stories like this are happening among God's people every day. A now example: Heidi last year shot to fame when she stood up in a German church while an imam intoned a Muslim prayer to Allah. "Jesus alone is Lord here!" she shouted. This weekend she is organising a human prayer chain of thousands to hold hands all the way round the borders of Germany. "Protect the borders of our nation, Lord," they will pray.

Presumption

But it's true, not every 'good idea' is a 'God idea', nor every need a call. How many times do we read of kings asking the Lord, "Shall I or shan't I go up against them?" The base line is, "Will You, Lord, be with us and

---

81   2 Kings 23:20, 1 Sam 14
82   *These are all warning markers — DANGER! — in our history books, written down so that we don't repeat their mistakes.* (1 Cor 10:11) Our positions in the story are parallel — they at the beginning, we at the end — and we are just as capable of messing it up as they were.

win the battle for us, or won't You? Is it Your will or not?"

King Jehoshaphat was a good King. His friend, the King of Israel, wanted Judah to join Israel in battle. "Let's ask God," says Jehoshaphat. The prophets come in and give their politically correct 'words'. Jehoshaphat isn't convinced. "Isn't there a genuine prophet?" The non-pc (politically incorrect) prophet is called and eventually gives a true vision. "Judah scattered without a shepherd." But despite hearing God's voice Jehoshaphat is persuaded (political niceties?) to support his mate. He lost his life for it.

> Presumption is disobedience, not hearing or heeding the voice of the Lord.

Presumption is disobedience – not hearing or heeding the voice of the Lord. Presumption is either overstepping your boundaries, or doing or assuming something that is not on God's heart or agenda. It could even be just a timing issue. Examine the motivation. Whom will it benefit, God or you? Whose kingdom will it build, yours or God's? Who will get the glory?

King Saul has had instructions from Samuel to prepare a sacrifice for next Saturday. Everything's ready, troops and people are gathered – waiting and waiting. The enemy is swarmed just over the hill, about to attack at any minute. But the prophet doesn't show. (These prophets are so unpredictable!) The people are getting fearful and restless. Some are already escaping over the border to hide. The troops are more and more fidgety and ill-tempered. Too many are on the verge of AWOL. Saul is losing control. This could be disastrous for his rule. But he can't go to battle before asking God's blessing, so he takes the bull by the horns (so to speak) and makes the sacrifice himself. He's just finished when Samuel turns up. *"I was losing my army from under me ... so I took things into my own hands." "That was a fool thing to do. You didn't keep your appointment with God ... as a result your kingly rule is falling to pieces."* (1 Sam 13:12–13)

Often our presumptions look so very logical, but that's all they are – living out of our mind instead of our spirit, rationale instead of faith.

It is essential that we get to know God's voice accurately and, as

David prayed for Solomon, have discernment and understanding, *rule with reverent obedience under God's instruction.*

Backlash

This is a word I hear often in the prayer movements. It's spoken in sepulchral tones of warning, often rising out of chasms of fear. Books have been written about it, collections of the disastrous things that can happen to people. I know the motive is well-meaning and protective. But wait a minute! I haven't found the word, or any example of backlash, anywhere in scripture. In fact I find the opposite. (Unless you want to cite Sceva's sons who were acting outside of their boundaries with no right to the Name. There were also the factors of no God-focus, and obedience.)

The seventy came back triumphant. *"Master, even the demons danced to your tune!"* (Interesting, it was His tune they'd been singing.) Jesus said, *"I know. I saw Satan fall, a bolt of lightning out of the sky. See what I've given you? Safe passage as you walk on snakes and scorpions, and protection from every assault of the Enemy. No one can put a hand on you. All the same, the great triumph is not your authority over evil, but in God's authority over you and presence with you."* (Lk 10:17–20)

You have as little to fear from an undeserved curse as from the dart of a wren or the swoop of a swallow. (Prov 26:2)

By no means am I saying the devil doesn't have power; he does, and I have a suspicion it increases proportionately to our fear.

BUT: *He* (Jesus) *stripped all the spiritual tyrants in the universe of their sham authority at the Cross and marched them naked through the streets. So don't put up with people pressuring* (intimidating) *you.* (Col 2:15) Note, Jesus calls it 'sham authority'. It's pretended, lying authority. Satan is still the Liar.

Remember my three expanding jurisdiction dreams in chapter 4. In the first I was timid, allowing Satan (the neighbour) to get away with things, not opposing him. Then when I did oppose him I was fearful that he would come back and take revenge. He didn't, and he won't. *Resist the devil and he will flee from you.* (Jas 4:7)

> *The Lord shall deliver me from every evil work and will preserve me into His heavenly kingdom.* (2 Tim 4:18 KJV)

Who's Terrified of Who?

Here is the other side of the coin. Satan is terrified of you. He would do anything to stop you from realizing how potent you are. He does not want you to 'get' who you are and the authority you have been given, because he knows he will be kicked out of his squatters' quarters.

"Holy Blood!"

In my novice years in Bali, villagers invited me to a midnight celebration where they would "do just like you do" – invite the spirits in – "and cry too". (They had watched as we prayed with Bible School students to receive the Holy Spirit.) With the dean's wife I went over to watch.[83] Nine people sat on a dais to receive 'ancestral' spirits while the priest rang bells and fanned incense. Sure enough tears began to manifest on the dais, and some trembling. "How different," I thought. "The Holy Spirit brings joy and light." These faces were screwed up with darkness. Suddenly a man leapt down from the dais right beside me with a blood-curdling scream and jagged sword which he attempted to plunge into his chest. By the powers now possessing him the *keris* made no impression on his flesh.

In fright I hurriedly stepped back muttering, "Blood of Jesus!" Some of the men in the crowd wrestled the sword off the man and handed it to another of the 'candidates' who repeated the performance. Meanwhile an old woman from the dais was now dancing in the yard. "Blood!" I heard, "Blood, blood, Holy Blood!"

"What was that?" I asked my friend and scurried forward again to find out. The old lady was standing in a trance, trembling from

---

[83] Do not, however, do what I did out of curiosity. Scripture forbids our being involved in any way in occult or idolatrous ceremonies and I would not do this today. God was merciful, understanding my ignorance of the dark spirit world in those days. He used it to teach me an unforgettable lesson.

head to toe and staring straight toward us. So far everything had been conducted in Balinese and therefore unintelligible to us, except for these two words in Indonesian. Next day I asked the villagers what that part was about blood. "No, nothing about blood." Then I realized that the spirits in the woman had seen the blood of Jesus applied to our lives and were trembling and crying out in terror. That was my first lesson in the power of the Blood of Jesus and how terrified the dark realm is of it.

Jesus said the devils believe and tremble. Often they may have more faith than we do!

I love the stories of Gideon and Rahab. Both stories are about God giving intelligence to His troops. In both instances the soldiers hear from the enemies' mouths how terrified they are and how certain of defeat at the hands of God's people. The good news galvanised God's people to fight vigorously and of course, win.

Some Cautions

There are cautions: *Now stay strong and steady. Obedient ... Hold tight to your God ... vigilantly guard your souls; Love God, your God. Because if you wander off and start taking up with these remaining nations ... know for certain that God, your God will not get rid of these nations for you. They'll be nothing but trouble to you – horsewhips on your backs and sand in your eyes ...* (Josh 23:6-13)

So, failure to love and obey God may result in your jurisdiction remaining under enemy occupation. In other words, if your jurisdiction is not responding to your rule and coming under the Lord's dominion check for these things. *You won't be able to face your enemies until you get rid of these cursed things.* (Josh 7:13)

Abdicating Jurisdictions

This can happen for all kinds of reasons and is happening all the time. Pilate, of course, is the classic example. He knew well his jurisdiction.

"*Do you not know I have power to crucify you and power to let you go?*" (Jn19:16 NKJV) But Pilate washed his hands, hoping that would exonerate him from what he was about to do. "*I am innocent of the blood of this just Person.*" (Mt 27:24 NKJV) **Wanting to gratify the crowd** *he delivered Jesus, after he had scourged him, to be crucified.* (Mk 15:15 NKJV)

King Zedekiah did something similar with Jeremiah. "Look he is in your hand. The king can do nothing to oppose you," he said to his parliament. So they took Jeremiah and cast him into the dungeon... *Zedekiah the king said to Jeremiah,* "**I am afraid of the Jews** *that they will deliver me to the Chaldeans and they will abuse me.*" *But Jeremiah said, "They shall not deliver you. Please obey the voice of the Lord which I speak to you. So it will be well with you and your soul shall live.*" (Jer 38:5, 19, 20 NKJV) He didn't obey, and was blinded and taken captive.

Eli was very old; and he heard everything his sons did to all Israel and how they lay with the women who assembled at the door of the Tabernacle. So he said to them, "Why do you do such things? No my sons! It is not a good report I hear. You make the Lord's people transgress. If a man sins against the Lord who will intercede for him?" (1 Sam 2:22-24)

They took no notice. But there was more. God spoke to Eli. "*Why do you honour your sons more than me, to make yourselves fat with the best of all the offerings of My people?*" (1 Sam 2:29) Privilege. Corruption. Self-serving. Then God spoke through Eli's young protégé, Samuel. "*His sons have made themselves vile and he did not restrain them.*" (1 Sam 3:13)

The result was, in one day he and his sons and his daughter-in-law died, his grandson Ichabod, 'the glory is departed', was born. God replaced the priesthood with Samuel.

This is a very sobering story. Our homes and families are under our jurisdiction and God holds us responsible to see that our children are disciplined and taught the very unpopular and old-fashioned concepts of honouring God and man, obedience. The spirit of the age is trying to obliterate such characteristics from our society. He must be opposed, preferably collectively. Parents and families are under great pressure and need courage and strength to hold their positions and continue to walk in their God-given and God-backed authority. Your home is a touchdown for Heaven on earth, a bastion of God's Kingdom here.

I think abdication is a prevalent problem. Many jurisdictions have been abdicated; many thrones remain unclaimed by rightful heirs, especially as secular authorities apply ever more restrictions and opposition. Abdication may be through ignorance. It may be through fear. It may be through lack of believing God could possibly have a responsible role for you.

It's the overcomer he grants to sit with Him on His throne. The Throne you occupy is over your jurisdiction, the area God has allocated to you. Sitting on the Throne with Him you cannot act apart from Him.

I pray you now have the courage to take your seat and rule your jurisdiction victoriously – with Christ.

~

Chapter 12
Requisite For Reigning
Romance

Did you ever dream about being a King, or a Princess? The incredible part is that it's true. It is God's dream for us, written in His scroll for us before time was. As we've seen, each one of us is called to sit on a throne and to reign alongside His Son in His kingdom.[84]

There is however a prerequisite to this royal position; there is a specific route to the Throne. This is a lesson I have had to repeat a number of times under the Lord's tutelage. Romance precedes ruling is the lesson. He is a most creative Teacher. He needed me to thoroughly understand that He loved me before I could effectively act as a Regent for Him.

Love is not only the key; it is the facilitator, the initiator, the power and the sustainer. Only from the place of intimately knowing Him can I speak on His behalf. ("How will your husband have his tea?" "Yes, milk and one sugar thanks, not too strong." I can't speak for him if I don't know him.)

The Lord has the best sense of humour. Although I found the 'me' focus embarrassing in His lessons, I came to realize He was talking to His Bride,

---

84 Here's the proof. 1 Pet 2:9; Rom 8:17; 2 Tim 2:12

not just to or about me. We are a collective Bride and He longs to get these messages across to her. I am sharing with you a condensed version of some of those lessons, because you are called to be part of this very loved Bride.

Warning. You may find some of this soppy! Guys, you will need to get used to it; you are part of the Lord's Bride. (After all, we gals have been 'Sons' for a long time!) [85]

In the Prologue, *'In the Body or Out of the Body?'*, I recorded the experience that started this whole journey for me – this revelation of our jurisdictions. After seeing my mountains and my city I was taken up a funnel of light and experienced the multiple facets of Christ the Fountain. The experience ended when He wrapped me about with Himself and His Light, and I was dissolved into Him. *No longer two; they become one flesh. This is a huge mystery and I don't pretend to understand it all,* Paul said. (Eph 5:30)

I can't say I do either, but the Lord is going to great pains to get His Bride to understand this mystery at the end of the Church Age, because she has only a short time left to make herself ready.

She will then present to Him the jurisdiction ('talent') He has entrusted to her – which is His inheritance in the saints.

Lesson 1   Loved To The Throne

After reading Song of Solomon 7:10-13, this is what happened:

> He bent over me and kissed me. I have never been kissed like that. "I have understood all along, Little One, the pain, the turmoil. I know how much you tried to please Me. I was there all the time, but You wouldn't receive My love. You were so anxiously looking 'out there' for Me. But I am right here, close. Relax and receive My love. Let Me love you. You have to accept My kisses. I shut off the 'buts' from your lips. Forget

> 'I am my Beloved's And His desire is toward me...'
> SoS 7:10 (NKJV)

---

[85] I debated about including some of the more intimate contents in this chapter, but had to concede that if I believed God was talking to His collective Bride I had no right to withhold part of the lesson. He is talking to you, Beloved.

everyone else. It's you and Me just now.

"You have sung to Me, Little One. Now let Me sing to you." (I can't hear anything. I'm tightening up with anxiety trying to hear – His Voice, His words, His tune.) But I sense that it's not with my ears, it's with my spirit (much as I'd like to hear with my ears). I sense an orchestra of angels gathering. The chief musician is striking up the music. A host is gathering and joining in, orchestra and choir. Then He chimes in with His solo. There are no words I hear or understand. But this is all for me! He is making sure I understand this is His command performance for me.

Next I find He has pulled me to Him and we are dancing in the middle of it all. It's like an enormous ballroom and the orchestra and choir, still performing, are also twirling and dancing together with us. He is really enjoying this, laughing and catching me to Him, releasing me, but His one hand never letting me go, gathering me up again joyously. The angels are having fun too. Then the crowd parts and we are dancing up a guard of honour formed by trumpeters.

"Where are we going?" I ask. We are dancing up a hill of light. He picks me up in His arms and carries me as though He is carrying me over the threshold of our bridal home. Then He sits down on the Throne on top of the rise with me on His knee. I have a bridal veil trailing off the back of my hair. I'm hanging my head embarrassed from all this public attention. He kisses me again on the mouth pushing my face up gently with the pressure of His lips, laughing. It's as though He's saying, "Get used to it. It's you I've chosen, and I'm going to love you unashamedly, even in public".

He doesn't speak, but as He holds me I instinctively know that I can't remain this shy little drooping Bride sitting on His knee. Somehow I am being transformed. Then the veil has come off and I am sitting tall beside Him on His Throne and a Crown is on my head.

> Accepting His love will turn me from a timid virgin into a Queen.

I understand that the only way to this incredible seat of authority and responsibility beside Him is through accepting the intimacy He has been lavishing on me. Accepting His love will turn me from a timid virgin into a Queen.

I cry at all this. It's quite overwhelming. His hand is brushing away my hair and my tears. "There is so much damage, Little One. Only by accepting My love can all the damage be healed. You see now why it had to be Me you answer to. No-one else can do this for you. I am jealous over you. Will You accept My love?"

"My Lord, I accept Your love. Please break the things that draw me back, the fear, the lack of trust, the hurt. I submit these to you."[86]

Lesson 2   Riding with Him

This Vision had three distinct scenes. I realize in retrospect that each one involved a different Person of the Godhead.

Scene 1. I was playing joyously with the Father in a meadow. He was on a seat and I was a small child romping carefree in the grass, accepted, loved and safe.

Scene 2. I was now a young woman sitting on Jesus' knee, and we were deeply in love. Then He placed me on the Throne beside Him, put a crown on my head, a ring on my finger and a sceptre in my hand and said, "All right, it's time to go now".

Scene 3. I'd been enjoying our time together and was reluctant to break up our intimacy. He climbed on a great white horse and I expected to climb on with Him, still close, but He said, "No, there's your horse". Next thing I was on my own horse beside Him. On the other side of me, hard up against mine was another horse. Its rider was the Paraclete.[87] We began to ride out and my horse started veering right while the Lord's veered left. I found I had no control of my horse; the Paraclete riding hard up against me had total control of him. This was distressing. "No! No!" I cried, "We must keep together."

---

86   JAA Journal Nov 14, 2002
87   Another name for the Holy Spirit, third Person of the Trinity.

"No," said the Paraclete, "this is the way it must be." So as we rode we diverged farther and farther from the Lord on His horse. Then I saw what we were doing. We were riding around a herd of beautiful stags, mustering them, the Lord to one side of them, the Paraclete and I to the other. Working together we gently herded them towards a pass and nudged them through into a new place.[88]

It reminded me of something Philip Hunt of *World Vision* had said: "*Let's get the herd all going in the same direction. That's one of the arts of leadership*". This is often how we influence our jurisdictions, imperceptibly nudging.

Some time later the Lord gently reprimanded me saying, "How come you remember the third part of the vision and forget the others? How come you don't think about the love scenes – how much you mean to Me? It's not so much what you do or achieve for Me; it's our relationship that means most to Me."

I was still hooked on the doing to be acceptable rather than the being. So there are more lessons yet. He's still working on a change of focus.

Lesson 3   My Bride

After reading Ezekiel chapter 16, I went to worship with the cry, "I can't imagine how You love me – the price You paid!" What developed was an unforgettable time of worship in which I was singing the Son's formal presentation of the Bride to the Father.

In brief it went something like this:

> Father, here is the Bride I have chosen.
> Please receive her into our home.
> She is the one I have chosen
> The one to share our Throne.
>
> I found her distraught by the roadside,
> beaten, abused, and abandoned —
> a discarded heap of ragged weeping.

---

88   JAA Journal. Vision, early 90's.

I loved her. Father I loved her.
I picked her up, but she fought Me.
She bit and scratched and spat.
Her actions were wild with fear.

But I loved her still,
loved her until
there was no more fight,
until she believed Me,
until she would let Me
cradle and comfort her,
wipe away the tears,
wash away the dirt,
and heal the wounds.

I paid the highest price,
great personal sacrifice.
Please, dear Father, accept her.

I've covered her with My robe.
She is the one I chose
to sit with Us on Our throne.

The one for whom I died,
Father,
I present —

My Bride.

Christ's love makes the church whole. His words evoke her beauty. Everything He does and says is to bring the best out of her. *Dressing her in dazzling white silk, radiant with holiness.* (Eph 5:26)

Lesson 4   **Love Letter**

He wrote me a Love Letter – to allay my fears and help me believe how much I mean to Him. He longed to be refreshed and ravished by my uninhibited love.

I responded incredulously.

I never believed You could love me like this – that it's ME You want. You look at me and catch Your breath. Your eyes are alight and dance with unashamed delight when You look at me. You beg me to sing for You; You're enraptured by my voice. Hang on its notes. Unbelievable! You have eyes only for me. I was Yours, betrothed from birth, and You have waited all this time. You've tried to show me. But I was blinkered by pain and rejection, choked up with the devil's lies: that I didn't measure up, wasn't worthy, was the last, least, bottom of the heap. And all the time You were saying, "Well done! You're my hero! It's you I choose".

I'm sorry I've been so hard to convince. Your love makes everything else inconsequential. I'm overwhelmed. I come alive, healed. I revel in Your love, chuckle with delight. Teach my passion to grow. Prize open the wells of my deepest being. Clear out the gunk, the rocks and rubble still blocking the pressure of this force from within me. Let it burst out like a powerful bore, gushing living waters of Love. You are my whole life and source. I LOVE YOU. Words are so inadequate, no song can tell it, no act an adequate response.

Help me! I've fallen irredemptibly in love and it's Your fault! I wouldn't have dreamt of it. It was You, courting me, wooing me, not giving up, loving on me, showing me things, whispering – till at last I could hear and believe You. You've been at it my whole life, stuck with it, never given up on me. That's love! And now that I've fallen so helplessly head-over-heels for You, You won't leave me, You won't turn away, You won't say 'that's enough', 'that's too much' or 'not what I meant' or 'wanted'. You

WANTED me with an insatiable persistent desire, proven over the years. You won't walk away. You will take me with you. Never alone again, never unvalued again, always precious, priceless, adorning You, making You proud. 'Gratitude' is an empty old tin can! What can I say? No language can ever be enough. I love You, I love You, I love You!

He is GOD. And we are His Bride, conquered by love, chosen before time, for eternity! How rich we are!

Finally

He beckons me. (This is you too, remember, the collective Bride.) He has a gold robe for me to put on. Don't crush it now with your big hugs! But it doesn't crush this magnificent gold thread, fine as silk. "Now close your eyes," He says. He is fastening a necklace around my neck. I finger crusted gems. "Wait, don't open them yet." Now I feel a weight gently placed on my head, adjusted. I can sense Him step back with a satisfied sigh. "Now?" "Yes now." I glance at Him first. Love and pride are pouring from His eyes. I am undone and bury myself in His chest, our arms clasping each other in a tight embrace. He disentangles me. "Want to see what I see?" He steps aside and I am there in a full-length mirror. I gasp with amazement, hardly able to look on the glory. It is dazzling me. It's hard for me to distinguish between Him and me, it's all so bright.[89]

"That's how you are to all who know how to see. Don't concern yourself with the blind. Leave them to Me."

He takes me by the hand. As we set off I reach to pick up my Moses rod. He gently takes it off me and hands me a

---

[89] Jesus said to the Father, The glory which You gave Me I have given them, I in them and You in Me. Jn 17:22–26 NKJV.

glistening sceptre. It is something between metal and light, tangible and not substance, but stronger than steel. I know it has no relation to substance as we know it, but can cut right through it. It can create, it can demolish, it can explode – it can do whatever is needed. There is nothing on earth that can resist it – or in heaven it seems.

At the top of the incline we sit on thrones, I on His right. Suddenly all of humanity is massed before us. It is almost like a haze of gold as we look out across all the nations from this elevated place.

"Lift your sceptre," He says. I do, and the whole mass bows.

"Woah, Lord!" I cry out. "I don't like this. This is just what Satan said to You: 'Bow to me and I'll give you the nations of the earth.'"

"It's because you bowed to Me, Joye, your sceptre is commanding them to bow to Me. The nations are Mine to give. Point over there."

I point and a stately man in colourful native costume stands and approaches the Throne. He kneels and takes off his crown, laying it at the feet of the King. When he looks up the King smiles and reaches out his arms. "My dear faithful friend," and they embrace long and warmly. "This is my wife," says the King to His friend. The chieftain kneels on one knee takes my hand and kisses it, smiling at my diamond ring. "An honour," he says, looking up into my eyes. In that look he is my friend too, warm and loyal and accepting.

"He has led His people to bow to Me, has stood with them and strengthened them through much pain and persecution at great personal cost. Your sceptre has helped him."

Just then a group of his people joins us in the Throne. "He will come later," the King says as the warrior returns to his other people. "There are others yet to bring."

I look over the great crowd and realize that my sceptre is designed to help them all in whatever ways are needed. The ultimate goal is to bring everything under the King's dominion, bowing at His feet and learning to reign with Him.[90]

~

The Lord is longing for intimacy with His Bride. "It's been so long, Darling!" His heart yearns for her and the consummation of His Love.

Do you sense what I sense? A stirring and a restlessness in Heaven as the Bridegroom and the hosts of heavenly beings, along with the *spirits of just men made perfect* (Heb 12:23) wait with bated breath for the cry, "Behold the Bridegroom is coming!" Earth, and the elements too, are restless, knowing the time is short.

Now let's take a look what He's promised to those who love Him.

~

---

90 JAA Journal 2007, PT

Chapter 13

The Culmination

'And Then I'll Marry You'

I'll marry you for good – forever!
I'll marry you in love and tenderness.
Yes, I'll marry you and neither leave you
nor let you go. You'll know me, God,
for who I really am. (Hos 2:19)

*For the time being He must remain out of sight in heaven **until** everything is restored to order again just the way God, through the preaching of his holy prophets of old, said it would be.* (Acts 3:20)

God has a long-range plan in which everything will be brought together and **summ**ed up in him, everything in deepest heaven, everything on planet earth. (Eph 1:9) That's the Mystery – the Grand Finale all creation is holding its breath for. That's con**summ**ation. Our relationship with the King is con**summ**ated in a marriage, and we are 'con**sum**ed' into Him.

You and I were written into the plan before God started sculpting the earth. God's focus was on the end, the 'culmination of all things', when

He brings everything together at the end of the age – that is: when time ends, when all the 'untils' become obsolete. (Time is just an earth concept – temporal. God's atmosphere is eternity.) *The created world itself can hardly wait for what's coming next. Everything in creation is more or less being held back.* God *reins it in until both creation and all the creatures are ready and can be released at the same moment into the glorious times ahead. Meanwhile, the joyful anticipation deepens.* (Rom 8:16-21)

Jesus said, *I am going to put it all together, pull it all together in a vast panorama.* (Mt 5:17) He talks about this happening in the 'fullness of times', explaining that the Holy Spirit has been given to us as a warranty until He comes to collect His purchase.[91] Both the Father and the Son paid an expensive price for this Bride, and the purchase hasn't been collected yet. Both parties have been preparing. The Bride has been making herself ready; and the wedding feast is being prepared.

The Long 'Until'

It's been a very long wait. The writer to the Hebrews describes it like this. *God said to His Son: "Sit alongside me here on my throne until I make your enemies a stool for your feet."* (Heb 1:13)

Then he sat down right beside God and waited for his enemies to cave in (to 'be made' his footstool. [NKJV]) (Heb 10:12,13)

It's still a sure thing! But you need to stick it out, staying with God's plan so you'll be there for the promised completion. (Heb 10:37) *God didn't put angels in charge of this business of salvation. It says in scripture, 'You put them (mankind) in charge of Your entire handcrafted world.' When God put them in charge of everything, nothing was excluded. But we don't see it yet, don't see everything under human jurisdiction.*(Heb 2:5-8)[92]

So what is it we're waiting for?

A lot of very invested people are watching our progress down here –

---

91 'redemption of the purchased possession'. Eph 1:9,10.
92 Heb 1:13; Heb 10:12,13

a great crowd of witnesses hanging out of heaven cheering us on. *Through acts of faith they toppled kingdoms, made justice work, took the promises for themselves... This means all these pioneers are cheering us on! No wonder!* (Heb 11:32; 12:1)

"Come on! Come on! Don't fall asleep; don't quit on the job. We don't want to wait another two thousand years!" Hebrews asks, *Do you see what this means – all these pioneers who blazed the way, all these veterans cheering us on? It means we'd better get on with it,* **because** *their lives of faith are not complete apart from ours!* (Heb 12:1, 40)

That revelation exploded in me. Dear God! I was in tears. He showed me how strategic we are at this end of the age. We're completing what the heroes of faith were believing God for. We all fit together across the arc of time, not complete without one another. And they are still waiting!

This is the visitation that brought the revelation:

Abraham's Visit

It was May 2009. I was in that half-awake state between sleep and wake, not yet engaged with the day, the time when it seems easier for God to talk to us. I was in an empty desert place standing at a wooden table and bench having just farewelled someone off to my left. To my right stood a stranger in long robes and a hooded cloak that concealed part of his face, so it was hard to see his features. "Would you like a cuppa?" I called, and he came over and sat down on the bench. I went off (who knows where in this desert place!), returning with a cup of tea and a generous slice of cake wrapped in clingwrap. The pastry end crumbled a little as I unwrapped it and I apologised (as I tend to do about my inferior offerings!). "I'm sorry my cake is a bit crumbly," I said, gesturing for him to help himself.

I was curious to know who he was, all hidden in his robes. So I looked up into his eyes and asked directly, "Are you Abraham?" Without answering he reached out his staff to my proffered morning tea and suddenly my offering went up in flames! I gasped – and froze! A fearful awe snatched my breath away. This was not just a nice little act of hospitality on my part. This was serious!

(Looking back, it's comforting to realize that my sacrifice was acceptable to God – by fire! We don't have to make grand offerings to be accepted; He made the only offering necessary for our acceptance. And just our ordinary every-day acts of service give Him pleasure.)

I was totally frozen. My first thought was, "Dear Lord! I've turned into a pillar of salt like Lot's wife out here in the desert!" But then I knew it wasn't salt; I was like a molten pillar of some kind. The man turned to move away. I called after him, "No, don't leave me, I can't move!" I tried to reach out, but couldn't. My mind was still trying to work out what molten substance I seemed to be – it wasn't gold, more like silver or crystal. The man continued to move away. I called out again. "Please don't go away. Don't leave me like this!"

He half turned and said, "You are part of the Foundations". My mind raced off again. "Foundations? Foundations of what? The Temple?" No, that wasn't it. "Was it the N...?"

Yes! It was the New Jerusalem!

At that instant the pillar that I was shot high into the air like a column of light and began to multiply out in identical pillars in both directions forming a wall of light, diminishing out towards the horizon – something like a wooden fence with abutting planks, but the planks were light. My substance was Light. The replications happened so fast the wall reached the horizon in an instant. (*The walls you're rebuilding are never out of my sight. Your builders are faster than your wreckers.* Isa 49:16)

At the same time God instantly downloaded scriptures about the New Jerusalem – *"Come here. I'll show you the Bride, the Wife of the Lamb."* He showed me Holy Jerusalem descending out of Heaven from God, *resplendent in the bright glory of God. The city shimmered like a precious gem, light-filled, pulsing light.* (Rev 21:10)

I saw Holy Jerusalem, new created, descending resplendent out of Heaven, as ready for God as a bride for her husband. (Rev 21:2)

Abraham looked for a City with real and eternal foundations – the city designed and built by God. (Heb 11:10)

I had the distinct impression that this city was forming **now** and we were part of it. I was dubious about this encounter. It didn't fit my 'theology'.

Then the Lord stumbled me upon Hebrews 11. It lists the Heroes of Faith including Abraham. Abraham was not remembered and listed in this hall of fame for his great exploits:
- taking a private army the length of Palestine to north of Damascus
- routing a conglomerate of kings
- retrieving his hapless nephew and his stolen goods
- or for any of his acts of faith-based obedience – like leaving his homeland in Iran, or sacrificing Isaac.

None of these examples of his taking charge of his jurisdiction earned him a citation on this list. Abraham was honoured for all time and God called him 'Friend', because he lived keeping his eye on the invisible city.

God is not impressed with the exploits we do for him, the battles we win, the enemies we route, the great displays we make; he is proud when, despite everything, our focus remains fixed on the invisible – His great plan of the ages – unwaveringly believing that He will do what He has promised.

I was struck by the fact that not one of these great men and women of faith in the Hebrews gallery 'received the end of their faith'. None received what they believed for, yet God was commending their faith. (My misguided judgment might have given it a fail grade!)

Still Waiting – For Us

But more astounding is why they didn't receive what they believed for. Hebrews goes on to say: **because without us they are not complete**! (Heb 11:40 NKJV) It definitely wasn't their lack of faith, or their misapplication of faith. It was ME!

Suddenly I was in tears. They need us! Abraham, who faithfully looked for an eternal city where God lived, Abraham the friend of God, was not complete without us! We, in our day, are finishing the end of his faith, completing the eternal city. *God had a better plan for us: that their faith and our faith would come together to make one completed whole, their lives of faith not complete apart from ours.*(Heb 11:40) Abraham at one end and we at the other end of the age are making God's magnificent plans complete. No wonder we're told we'd better get on with it.

I was overwhelmed at how significant this generation is at the end of the age! Not one of us is without significance. We are the completion of God's dream as He gathers everything together for His Son. We are His inheritance.

The intimacy and the reigning is all training for the Royal Marriage.

The Eternal City

The anticipated New Jerusalem had, for me, been more than a thousand years away – some far-off, incomprehensible cubic structure that would one day hover over geographic Jerusalem, or replace it. It was too way out there to think about, just perhaps to dream how wonderful it would be – one day. And to be honest my imagination had it a lot more literal than what was now being presented. I was sceptical of this new idea yet my spirit remained excited.

My friend, a life-coach to Christian movements, reassured me with this verse. *I'll make each conqueror a pillar in the sanctuary of my God, a permanent position of honour. Then I'll write names on you, the pillars: the Name of my God, the Name of God's City – the New Jerusalem coming down out of Heaven – and my new Name.* (Rev 3:12)

The City is the Bride

If the city is the Bride, then certainly she is on earth now, preparing. That's us!

So the promises are not way off in a distant future. The New Jerusalem, the glorious city of God, is current here and now. We are part of it – preparing for it to be revealed – preparing the Bride for her soon arriving Bridegroom!

The Light City

This is the 'Bride all light within'. The city[93] is nothing like my early concepts. It is a city of Light in which is no shadow or darkness. It is forming in the midst of, and despite, a people of gross darkness, and we, God's redeemed children, are the lights who are forming it.[94] God uses so many metaphors to try to describe the facets of spiritual things that are outside our finite comprehension! The city and the Bride are the same thing. We are it.

New Jerusalem is the capital city of God's invisible Kingdom for which we are currently operating as regents. It is the city that God is building with us in these last times. Now at the end of the Age it is forming across the earth. The message that Abraham brought was that we are foundational to what his whole life was looking for! Incredible!

This city is a living vibrant entity. Its connections are light-connections, its walls and edifices are light. The city is rising across the whole globe, covering the earth as the waters cover the sea. God's light people are connecting in the Spirit, forming this amazing structure not made with hands or organization.

Do you see what we've got? An unshakable kingdom! ... brimming with worship. (Heb 12:18,22) *If the makeshift government of Moses' time (it's 'dazzling inaugural' lighting Moses' face as blindingly as the sun) impressed us, how much more this brightly shining government installed for eternity?* (2 Cor 3:11)

To catch a glimpse of how awesome this city is that we're building, look at this:

> *You didn't come to Mt Sinai – all that volcanic blaze and earthshaking rumble. You've come to Mt Zion, the city where the living God resides. The invisible Jerusalem is populated by throngs of festive angels and Christian citizens. It is the city where God is Judge ... His voice that time shook the earth to its foundations. This time – He's told us this quite plainly – He'll also rock the heavens. One last shaking getting*

---

93 Take a look at the amazing description of the city in Isa 54:11–17.
94 Isa 61 goes into detail about the Light of God arising on His people.

rid of all the historical and religious junk so that the unshakable essentials stand clear and uncluttered. (Heb 12:22, 27)

We won't be immune to the shakings, but God says because we hung in there – *I'll keep you safe in the time of testing that will be here soon, and all over the earth, every man woman and child will be put to the test. I'm on my way; I'll be there soon. Keep a tight grip on what you have so no one distracts you and steals your crown.* (Rev 3:10–12) That's focus again.

Here are some of the things Isaiah and Jeremiah saw about the New Jerusalem: it is the new Ark, God's Throne, a refuge city, a place of comfort and safety – *nothing to fear; far from terror; it won't even come close!*[95]

We spirit beings live and operate from this impregnable light city, reconnecting people with God, releasing prisoners, bringing liberty and joy (Isa 61), fulfilling our mandates in our jurisdictions. It is growing apparent that in these days of increasing darkness God's children across the globe are learning to live in this dimension, knowing that what happens to their physical bodies can't reach their spirit beings. (Inspiring testimonies of saints faithful to death are coming from many parts of the globe.)

Live As Though You Are In It

I was impressed with a note about Abraham. *By an act of faith he lived in the country promised him ... Isaac and Jacob did the same* (his children and grandchildren). *Abraham did it by keeping his eye on an unseen city, with real, eternal foundations – the City designed and built by God. If they were homesick for the old country, they could have gone back any time they wanted. But they were after a better country than that – heaven country. You can see why God is so proud of them, and has a City waiting for them.* (Heb 11:8,16)

---

95 Isa 54:11ff; Isa 49:12; Jer 3:17; Isa 66:13,18.

[I paid a memorable visit to the Oaks of Mamre, near Hebron, where Abraham by faith occupied the Promised Land. It was there he entertained God and His two companions, there he received His covenant promises of the Seed and the Land, and there He contended with God for Sodom and his nephew Lot. When I attempted to pay a second visit to Mamre I discovered it is now in hostile territory and no longer accessible. There is an enemy agenda to steal the inheritance and to prevent God's plan, both in the natural and spiritual dimensions.]

And so we live as though we are in it, bringing all the blessings and glory of this city into our jurisdictions.

What has this to do with our jurisdictions?

This battle to take back and maintain territory will continue. Our jurisdictions are spiritual, invisible territories, our spheres of influence. I believe God wants us to be conscious of the city forming and to live from this spiritual position. We are collectively bringing our jurisdictions under the Lord's dominion. We are forming an invisible spiritual dimension over our spheres of influence.

I see a globe-covering city forming as Light connects our various jurisdictions. This is where I live by faith as Abraham did – in the city of Light God is building in the earth.

And for the time being the Bridegroom remains out of sight until... *Eventually the holy people of the High God will be given the kingdom and have it ever after – yes forever and ever.* **When the court comes to order** *the horn*[96] *will be stripped of its power and totally destroyed. Then the royal rule and the authority and the glory of all the kingdoms under heaven will be handed over to the people of the High God. Their rule will last forever. All other rulers will serve and obey them.* (Dan 7:18, 26)

Of the increase of His government and peace there will be no end, to order and establish His Kingdom with judgment and justice forever. (Isa 9:7 NKJV)

---

96 The final evil world power.

Conclusion

So there is a glorious conclusion to bringing God's order in our jurisdictions.

In a Nutshell:

> Your jurisdiction is – the area over which you have legal right to speak, the area God has portioned you influence over.
>
> Your role is – to establish God's dominion or lordship over it, on earth as it is in heaven.
>
> The goal is – to restore the King's inheritance back to Him, to prepare the way for the King's return.
>
> The purpose – to complete what the heroes of faith laboured for, to fulfil God's dream of a Bride for His Son.

Ultimately, your jurisdiction and mine, and all the myriad jurisdictions over which God's children have taken charge, are being gathered up to complete a Kingdom whose dominion will know no boundary, nor end. Reigning over this infinite empire will be the King and His long-awaited Bride.

Isaac Watts puts it exquisitely in his 1719 anthem:[97]

> *Jesus shall reign where're the sun*
> *Does his successive journeys run;*
> *His kingdom stretch from shore to shore,*
> *Till moons shall wax and wane no more.*

---

97 (3 out of 14 verses)

Great God, whose universal sway
The known and unknown worlds obey,
Now give the kingdom to Thy Son,
Extend His power, exalt His throne.

The sceptre well becomes His hands;
All Heav'n submits to His commands;
His worship and His fear shall last
Till hours, and years, and time be past.

~

The End

About the Author

Joye Knauf Alit

(Need some pronunciation help?
KNAUF: k.now.f – ALIT: 'A' as in father,
'lit' as in lick. The accent is on the first syllable.)

Joye was born in New Zealand to pioneering Pentecostal parents and became 'automatically part of the team'! Her grandparents on both sides were also credentialed ministers with the Assemblies of God in its infancy in that nation (AW Thompson long-term superintendent). Joye acknowledges that she was surrounded and nurtured by apostles.

From the age of three her ambition was to be a missionary and in Primary School she was already organizing prayer meetings and evangelistic outreaches. With this missions focus she trained as a teacher (pioneering the Evangelical Union in her college). From the age of 21 (except for five years in the Maori revival in NZ's King Country) she spent 27 years in Indonesia, mainly in Bali. She trekked mountain trails to bring the Gospel to unreached peoples, taught in Bible Colleges, pioneered Children's Homes, Foundations, a training school, churches, ministers' prayer fellowships, children's ministries, and has experienced revivals. She has twice seen the dead raised. ("I didn't mean to raise the dead," says Joye. "I just didn't know what else to do than pray in the Spirit.")

Now based in Australia she is a credentialed minister with the Global Apostolic Network. She coördinated the British Reconciliation events in SE Qld, Australia, was editor of PrayerLink for the South Pacific, has been involved in the All Pacific Prayer Movement, the AD2000 Movement (leading a team to Mt Kailash in coördination with Wagner's Everest initiative), and is still active in Global prayer initiatives and training internationally.

Joye is a vibrant 70+-year-old, plugged into the Source of Life. She is a God-carrier and a Joy-bringer. 'Jealous for Jesus', Joye says, "Show me the places where

Jesus has never been named and other gods have received all the praise; I will worship Him there. The earth and its peoples are HIS." Joye's passion to present them back to Him has taken her into some of the remotest areas of the globe to exalt King Jesus and open the way for His Kingdom. To Joye, God's Word is the living and powerful source of her inspiration and energy, but not more than her relationship with its Author with whom she has an intimate day by day relationship.

Having seen enemy plans demolished, courses of nations changed, lives and territories transformed, as well as many now serving God in the Nations, Joye expects this to be the footprint of the church in any society.

Joye has three daughters and 7 grandchildren between Brisbane and Auckland.

Joye leads Jubilaté Ministries and may be contacted at
jubilatemin@gmail.com or
jurisdictions4you@gmail.com

www.ingramcontent.com/pod-product-compliance
Lightning Source LLC
Chambersburg PA
CBHW070615300426
44113CB00010B/1542